BOOST
your company's profits

THOROgOOD

THE PUBLISHING BUSINESS
OF THE HAWKSMERE GROUP

To Philippa... with more love than ever...

Published by Thorogood Limited

12 -18 Grosvenor Gardens

London SW1W ODH

Thorogood Limited is part of the
Hawksmere Group of Companies.

A CIP catalogue record for this book is available from the British Library.

ISBN 1 85418 136 X (trade edition)

ISBN 1 85418 156 4

Printed in Great Britain by Ashford Colour Press

Designed and typeset by Paul Wallis at Thorogood

Preface

Accountants seem to have a knack of making finance and accounting complicated. It is almost as though they want to preserve a mystique. Yet in the competitive business world of today, the profit-driven manager needs practical techniques to use every day. The common denominators of business are people, profit and cash flow.

The book provides and illustrates the practical finance and accounting techniques needed to manage for profit, for boosting profit and to generate the **maximum** cash flow from a business. It will benefit everyone from management trainees to departmental managers, technical specialists to managing directors, who may have got the top job despite their lack of financial know-how. People managing their own business, whether it is a company or a professional partnership, will find the book particularly valuable. Qualified accountants will find it helpful to learn how to communicate more effectively with non-financial colleagues.

The keynote is simplicity. The approach is to explain essential finance and accounting using street language. There is no place for unexplained jargon. Techniques are illustrated with the help of practical examples. The book contains what the driven manager needs to know. What is not needed has been deliberately omitted. There is no attempt to pursue accounting purity at length, merely for the sake of technical correctness.

The book is divided into four parts:

■ the first one explains the essential knowledge needed to understand financial language. Otherwise, finance is as confusing as trying to understand cricket without any knowledge of the rules. Every manager needs to be able to read and interpret profit-and-loss accounts and balance sheets. Ratio analysis is explained and illustrated, because this reveals the financial performance and well-being of a business, or conversely may provide an early warning of impending disaster unless urgent action is taken.

Many people work for companies whose shares are quoted on a stock exchange. Different ratios are used to evaluate the financial performance of a listed company and these can have substantial effect on the share price. Failure to perform adequately may even result in a takeover by a predator, followed by painful rationalisation and redundancies. So it is important to know and understand the yardsticks by which companies listed on a stockmarket are judged.

- the second part concentrates entirely on turning round loss making companies, because survival depends on tackling this urgently and effectively.

- the third part deals with the practical techniques needed to improve profits, cash flow and return on investment this year. The essentials of budgeting, monthly reporting and year-end forecasting are described. Cash management techniques are explained in detail. The anatomy of profitability is revealed, to provide the insight needed to optimise current-year profits. The financial-analysis techniques for effective decision-making are covered. Project evaluation, capital expenditure, make v by and lease v buy decision-making are explained.

- the final part deals with developing the business to grow profits and cash flow dramatically. It shows how to adopt the quantum-leap mentality; how to turn idle dreams into a written vision for outstanding success; and then how to take the action needed to make it a reality.

To ensure the contents of this book are as jargon free as possible, a glossary of terms is provided at the end of the book. Terms printed in **bold lettering and underlined** in the text are to be found in the glossary.

This is not a book merely to be read and enjoyed. It is a book to be used continuously. It has been written expressly to provide practical help to improve significantly profits, cash flow and return on investment.

Barrie Pearson

About the author

Barrie Pearson is Executive Chairman of Livingstone Guarantee plc, which he founded in 1976 and is based in London. Livingstone Guarantee provides help and advice on acquisitions, disposals, management buy-outs and buy-ins, stock market flotations and corporate finance. Clients range from household name multi-nationals to major financial institutions and private companies.

After graduating in Theoretical Chemistry, Barrie worked for Dexion Comino International as a line manager. Next he joined the Corporate Finance staff of The Plessey Company, and subsequently became financial controller of Plessey Micro-Electronics, a worldwide business made up of eleven divisions. Then he was appointed Group Commercial Development Executive of The De La Rue Company, responsible for acquisitions and divestments. He has worked extensively in Europe, the USA and the Far East.

Barrie has written eight books on various business topics, including *The Shorter MBA*. Many of his articles have been published in business magazines in the UK, Europe and the USA.

Contents

part

Understanding the essentials

Three
Performance-ratio analysis

Four
Stockmarket ratio analysis

part

2

Turning round loss-making companies

part

How to boost profits this year

part 4

How to achieve dramatic growth in profits

Ten

Understanding
the essentials

The profit-and-loss account

The profit-and-loss account that companies are required to publish annually shows more than merely the profit or loss for the financial year.

Contents of the profit-and-loss account

- turnover
- some information on costs
- bank interest, payable and receivable
- taxation payable
- dividends to shareholders
- profit retained in the business to finance expansion

In essence, the profit or loss is calculated by:

the sales turnover or fee income invoiced, but not necessarily paid by customers, during the year

less the total of

the costs incurred to produce the invoiced sales turnover or fee income, but not necessarily paid during the year

and

the **depreciation** charged on assets owned within the business during the year.

It is inevitable that the profit made by a business and the amount of cash generated will be different, because the profit-and-loss account is not based upon cash received and paid out during the financial year. Indeed, a profitable manufacturing company may consume cash during a period of expansion, because additional finance may be needed for:

- increased stocks of raw materials and finished goods

- the increased level of work-in-progress in the factory

- a larger amount of money owed by customers, which is described as debtors

- investment in capital equipment.

It would be understandable to assume that there is a standardised format for all profit-and-loss accounts, but it would be wrong. The presentation is broadly similar, but it is important not to be confused by different presentations.

Perhaps the simplest form of published profit-and-loss account is as shown in the spread sheet opposite.

For the year ending 31 December 1998

	1998 £m	1997 £m
Turnover	603	570
Operating costs	540	515
Operating profit	63	55
Net interest payable	(9)	(12)
Profit on ordinary activities before taxation	54	43
Taxation on profit of ordinary activities	14	12
Profit attributable to ordinary shareholders	40	31
Dividends	13	10
Retained profit transferred to reserves	27	21

The published profit-and-loss account and the balance sheet need to be read in conjunction with the accounting policies and the notes to the accounts that accompany them in the **Annual Report** of each company.

The accounting policies explain the basis on which the accounts have been prepared, for example the method used to value stocks and work-in-progress.

The notes to the accounts provide the detail behind some of the figures shown in the profit-and-loss account and balance sheet, together with other supplementary information, for example details of directors' remuneration.

Typical descriptions of the terms used in the profit-and-loss account shown on page 5 are:

Turnover

Sales invoiced to customers during the financial year, excluding value-added tax (VAT). Only sales to third parties are taken into account for the profit-and-loss account of a group.

Operating costs

Consist of several items such as:

■ costs of goods and services invoiced

■ distribution costs

■ research and development

■ administrative and other expenses

■ employees' profit-sharing bonus.

Operating profit

Is the profit on the normal trading activities of the company, before taking into account bank interest and taxation.

Net interest payable

Is the net amount of interest receivable and payable on all overdrafts, loans, deposits and finance leases (as opposed to property leases).

Profit on ordinary activities before taxation

The 'profit before tax', but the use of the word ordinary is deliberate because there may be exceptional items as well, which will be explained later.

Taxation on profit on ordinary activities

Is based on the profit for the year and takes into account deferred taxation which arises from timing differences between the taxation rules and accounting policies used by the company. These timing differences are commonplace, eg. between capital allowances for taxation and depreciation, but disappear eventually. So deferred tax is provided for in the accounts only if it is expected to be payable. For example, this could arise on the disposal of fixed assets where the amount of taxation allowances claimed to date and the depreciation charged in the profit-and-loss account differ.

Profit attributable to ordinary shareholders

Profit earned for the ordinary shareholders, after charging the liability for taxation arising on the profits.

Dividends

The total cost of the dividend paid to ordinary shareholders.

Retained profit transferred to reserves

Profit after tax left in the business to provide additional finance for future growth and development.

Published profit-and-loss accounts often seem more complicated in real life. The only difference, however, is that other situations have arisen which need to be explained. They are really no more difficult to understand. Consider the profit-and-loss account shown on page 8:

For the year ending 31 December 1998

	Notes*	1998 £m	1997 £m
Sales turnover		**11,699**	11,123
Costs and overheads less other income	4	**(10,229)**	(9,826)
Operating profit	4	**1,470**	1,297
Exceptional items before taxation	5	**162**	157
Net interest expense	6	**(162)**	(142)
Profit on ordinary activities before taxation		**1,470**	1,312
Tax on profit on ordinary activities	7	**(531)**	(504)
Profit on ordinary activities after taxation		**939**	808
Dividends	9	**(341)**	(277)
Transfer to reserves		**598**	531

*The note references are shown in the profit-and-loss account, but the notes relating to accounts have not been reproduced here.

The items in this profit-and-loss account which may need some explanation are as follows:

Costs and overheads less other income

Is described as the operating costs of the business less other income such as government grants and royalties.

Exceptional items before taxation

These include items such as the profit or loss on disposal of fixed assets or the disposal of operations (businesses). One-off items to be included if appropriate are environmental provisions and reorganisation costs.

Depreciation

Depreciation is charged on tangible fixed assets, excluding land, and **intangible assets** owned by a company. It is included as part of the operating costs. The most commonly used method to calculate depreciation is to write off the cost of the asset evenly over its estimated useful life, taking into account any residual value likely to be realised on disposal, where appropriate.

The estimated useful life of assets may be considerably less than the period for which they are physically usable.

This applies particularly to electronic equipment. For example, a computer could still be usable after 10 years, but the company is likely to choose depreciation on the assumption that it will wish to buy a more technologically advanced machine much sooner.

Depreciation does not necessarily adjust the recorded value of the asset to reflect the market or realisable value. An obvious example is the purchase of a motor car, because immediately the vehicle is driven away from the showroom the value of the tax charged on a new car has been lost. Another example is a piece of custom-built electronic equipment designed to test a particular product. The realisable value would be only the scrap value of the individual parts, assuming that it could not be used or adapted by another company.

It must be realised that the provision of depreciation as part of operating costs does not involve setting cash aside to replace the asset in due course. It is simply 'book-keeping entries' in the financial records of the company.

Companies usually define a specific useful life to be assumed for depreciating different types of fixed assets. Typically these are:

Freehold buildings	25-60 years
Computer equipment	3-5 years
Plant and equipment	5-20 years
Motor vehicles	3-8 years

Consider the annual depreciation charge on computer equipment which cost £140,000 where the company assumes a useful life of five years and no residual value to be realised on disposal.

The annual depreciation charge will be one-fifth of the purchase price, ie. £140,000 divided by 5, which is £28,000 a year.

Internal profit-and-loss accounts

Other terms which may occur in profit-and-loss accounts prepared for internal use within a company include:

■ cost of sales

■ gross profit

■ bad-debt provision.

Gross profit

The gross profit is calculated as:

	£m
Sales turnover	3,372
less	
Costs of sales	(2,164)
equals	
Gross profit	**1,208**

Cost of sales

The cost of sales is more accurately described as the cost of goods and services invoiced. It is calculated as:

	£m
Value of stock and work-in-progress at beginning of financial year	430
plus	
Goods purchased and production costs incurred	2,248
less	
Value of stock and work-in-progress at end of financial year	(514)
equals	
Cost of sales	**2,164**

The selling and distribution costs, administration expenses and other operating costs are deducted from gross profit to calculate the operating profit.

Bad-debt provision

If a customer has gone into receivership or liquidation, and if there is no chance of receiving even partial payment of an outstanding debt, then the debt must be written off and charged to the profit-and-loss account.

At the end of each financial year, an estimate must be made of the eventual cost of likely bad debts as well as those actually written off. Accountants refer to these estimated amounts as provisions.

The charge to the profit-and-loss account each year is calculated by:

	£'000
Bad-debt provision at end of year	52
plus	
Bad debts written off	17
less	69
Bad-debt provision at start of year	45
Charged to profit and loss account	24

This may seem thoroughly confusing, but it is not. Bad debts of £17,000 have occurred during the financial year. In addition, the estimated amount of provision for likely bad debts has been increased by £7,000, from £45,000 to £52,000. So the total charge to the profit-and-loss account is £17,000 plus £7,000, namely the £24,000 shown.

Dividend payment

Dividends of stock-market-listed companies are usually paid twice a year. An interim dividend is paid after the half-year results are announced. The directors recommend a final dividend, which is paid to shareholders after they give their approval at the annual general meeting. Many private companies either choose not to pay a dividend at all, or alternatively are likely to pay only a final dividend.

If the dividend is, say, 1.0p per share, then income tax is deducted at the standard rate.

When this rate is 20%, the shareholder receives:

- a net dividend payment of 0.80p per share

and

- a **tax credit** of 0.20p per share.

On the quarter dates, 31 March, etc. and the company's year end, following the payment of any net dividend to shareholders, the company is required to pay to the Inland Revenue the value of the tax credits as a payment of advanced corporation tax. This can be claimed by the company setting it off against future corporation tax payments. It should be noted, however, that the Government has announced plans to abolish advanced corporation tax for dividends paid on or after 6 April 1999.

The actual amount of income tax payable by the shareholder on the dividend is adjusted annually by the Inland Revenue, for those who either are liable for the higher rate of income tax or are not liable to pay any income tax at all because of their low income. This is done as a result of the shareholder being required to declare net dividends and tax credits on his or her personal income-tax-return form.

The balance sheet 2

The balance sheet of a company published in the Annual Report provides a financial picture of the company at the end of the financial year, showing in essence:

■ the assets and liabilities of the company

and

■ the sources and amounts of finance used.

It should be realised, however, that the balance sheet at the end of a financial year may give a quite different picture compared to one prepared at other times during the financial year. For example, consider a manufacturing company supplying gift items, with peak sales at Easter and Christmas. Stock levels are likely to be at their lowest in, say, February and October when goods have been shipped to wholesalers and retailers in readiness for the selling season. The overdraft is likely to be lowest in, say, April and December when customers have paid for their orders received in time for the peak sales periods.

Many business executives find the balance sheet much harder to understand than the profit-and-loss account. Some give up the attempt, assuming that the balance sheet is of little importance. This is completely wrong! Assets must be managed as aggressively as profits, and the starting point for asset management is a thorough understanding of balance sheets.

It would be convenient if one could safely assume that every balance sheet has an identical format, but reality is that balance sheets only have similar formats.

A simple balance sheet may have the format shown below:

Balance sheet at 30 June 1998

	1998 £m	1997 £m
Fixed assets	407	351
Current assets	177	167
Creditors – due within one year	(149)	(147)
Net current assets	28	20
Total assets less current liabilities	435	371
Creditors – due after more than one year	(91)	(133)
	344	238
Called-up share capital	44	44
Reserves	300	194
	344	238

The same balance sheet could be presented using a different format:

Balance sheet at 30 June 1998

	1998 £m	1997 £m
Assets employed		
Fixed assets	407	351
Current assets	177	167
Total assets	584	518
Creditors due within one year	(149)	(147)
Net current assets (and liabilities)	28	20
Total assets less current liabilities	435	371
Financed by		
Creditors due after more than one year	91	133
Called-up share capital	44	44
Reserves	300	194
Total capital and reserves	344	238
	435	371

The differences between the two formats are that in the second one:

- creditors due after one year – is moved to the lower 'half' of the balance sheet

- net current assets – is listed as an extra, or 'memorandum', line into the layout of the balance sheet

A description of the above terms follows.

Fixed assets

Include land, buildings, plant, equipment, fixtures and fittings. Fixed assets are stated at cost, less accumulated depreciation, or may be included at a professional valuation in the case of land and buildings.

Current assets

Consist of :

- raw materials and finished goods, stocks, plus work-in-progress

- debtors – ie. amounts owed to the company by clients or customers

- deposits and short-term investments

- cash.

Creditors due within one year

Consists of:

- short-term borrowings, such as over-drafts

- current instalments of loans

- other creditors, eg. amounts owed by the company to suppliers, to share-holders (dividends), and the Inland Revenue.

Net current assets

Are current assets

less

creditors due within one year.

Creditors due after more than one year

Usually consist mainly of:

- secured and unsecured loans

- obligation under **finance leases** for the purchase of fixed assets.

Called-up share capital

Consists of ordinary, and in some cases, preference shares as well; both valued at nominal value. Share options are excluded until the shares are actually allotted to directors and staff.

Reserves

Consist of:

■ retained profits

and where appropriate

■ share premium account

■ property revaluation.

Each of these items is explained below:

Retained profits

All of the profit retained in the company (after the payment of corporation tax and dividends) to provide additional finance, since the formation of the company.

Share-premium account

the total premiums received in excess of the nominal value for all shares issued at higher than nominal value, after deducting the expenses of issuing them eg. when shares are issued as purchase consideration for an acquisition.

Property revaluation

The increase in value over the figure included in the balance sheet arising from a professional valuation of land and buildings by a qualified property surveyor.

Real-life balance sheets often present more detailed information. A familiarity with the basic layout of a balance sheet, however, means that the detailed balance sheet is just as easy to understand. An actual consolidated balance sheet illustrates this (shown overleaf).

Consolidated Balance Sheet of a Group (of companies)

at 30th September 1998

	1998 £m	1998 £m	£m	1997 £m
Fixed assets				
Intangible assets – brands		588.3		608.0
Tangible assets		3,279.4		2,725.2
Investments		206.1		177.2
		4,073.8		3,510.4
Current assets				
Stocks	761.1		733.7	
Debtors	873.5		827.5	
Cash at bank and in hand	137.8		113.4	
	1,772.4		1,674.6	
Creditors due within one year				
Borrowings	186.7		329.7	
Other creditors	1,301.3		1,166.3	
Net current assets		284.4		178.6
Total assets less current liabilities		4,358.2		3,689.0
Creditors – due after more than one year				
Borrowings	702.4		1,141.9	
Other creditors	162.6		103.3	
		865.0		1,245.2
Provisions for liabilities and charges		55.1		70.4
		3,438.1		2,373.4
Called-up share capital		442.5		440.9
Reserves				
Share premium account	7.2		425.8	
Revaluation reserve	664.8		(7.7)	
Special reserve	282.0		–	
Profit-and-loss account	2,010.2		1,486.1	
		2,964.2		1,904.2
		3,406.7		2,345.1
Minority shareholders' interests		31.4		28.3
		3,438.1		2,373.4

Items which may need some explanation in the opposite consolidated balance sheet are:

Intangible assets

Some companies include in the balance sheet a valuation of brand names acquired by the purchase of businesses from other companies.

The accounting policy adopted by some companies for including brands in the balance sheet is that significant owned brands acquired, the value of which is not expected to diminish in the foreseeable future, are recorded in the balance sheet as fixed intangible assets. No depreciation is provided on these assets but their value is reviewed annually and the cost written down as an exceptional item where permanent diminution in value has occurred.

Tangible assets

Fixed assets are stated at cost, after deducting government grants, or at professional valuation. Cost includes interest, net of any tax relief, on capital employed in major developments.

Investments

Consist of:

■ investments in associates, with a shareholding of up to 50%, which are valued at the cost of the shares, less **goodwill** written off on acquisition, plus the Group's share of retained profits and reserves since the date of acquisition

■ investments in other companies which are valued individually at the lower of cost or net realisable value. For listed shares, net realisable value is the market value of the shares. For unlisted shares, eg. in a private company, net realisable value is estimated by the directors.

Stocks

Consist of:

■ raw materials and consumables

■ work in progress

■ finished goods and goods for resale.

Stocks are valued at the lower of Group cost or net realisable value. No interest is included but, where appropriate, cost includes production and other direct overhead expenses.

Debtors

Are primarily trade debtors, ie. amounts owed by customers.

Provisions for liabilities and charges

Obligations such as payments to the staff-pension scheme and deferred taxation.

Special reserve

Is an item not commonly encountered. It might be described as a technical adjustment to the balance sheet. The share-premium account has been reduced by a transfer to an undistributable special reserve, following a special resolution passed by shareholders and confirmed by court order

Minority shareholders' interests

Is the value of that part of the subsidiary companies owned by minority sharehold-ers directly in the subsidiary, rather than by the Group.

Other creditors (due within one year)

Consist of items such as:

- trade creditors, ie. amounts owed to suppliers
- corporate taxation
- ordinary dividend payable
- current-year obligations under finance leases for the purchase of assets.

Goodwill

Goodwill merits an explanation although it is encountered only occasionally on a balance sheet. On the acquisition of a business, where the price paid exceeds the value of the net assets acquired, then the difference is treated as goodwill. Many companies write off goodwill against the reserves in the year of acquisition and so it does not appear on the balance sheet.

Research and development

Research and development is an item which occurs infrequently on a balance sheet, because most companies write off the expenditure in the year in which it is incurred as a charge to the profit-and-loss account, rather than capitalise it as an asset on the balance sheet.

Cash flow statement

UK companies are required to publish a consolidated cash flow statement annually, in addition to a profit-and-loss account and balance sheet.

The cash flow statement shows:

- cash flow from operating activities:
  - returns on investments and servicing of finance ie. net interest
  - taxation
  - capital expenditure
  - acquisitions and disposals
  - equity dividends paid
  - the sum of the above items is the net cash inflow or outflow before financing
- management of liquid resources for example, short-term deposits made or withdrawn
- financing
  - issue of shares increased or decreased of debt
- the net of all the above items is the increase or decrease in cash in the year.

An actual example of a consolidated cash flow statement will reveal the simplicity of a cash flow statement.

	1998 £m	1997 £m
Cash flow from operating activities	1,621	1,636
Return on investments and servicing of finance	(217)	(175)
Taxation	(429)	(474)
Capital expenditure and financial investment	(637)	(591)
Acquisitions and disposals	606	(1,361)
Equity dividends paid	(580)	(635)
Cash inflow/(outflow) before use of liquid resources and financing	364	(1,600)
Management of liquid resources	385	(336)
Financing		
• issue of shares	287	311
• (decrease/increase of debt)	(1,086)	1,267
Decrease of cash in the year	(50)	(358)

The cash flow from operating activities includes:

■ the profit before interest and tax

■ depreciation

■ profit or loss on sale of tangible fixed assets

■ share of profits and losses on dividends from associates (companies where the maximum group share ownership is 50%)

■ profit on disposal of subsidiaries and investments

■ movements of provisions of liabilities and charges

■ change in inventories, debtors and creditors.

Performance ratio analysis

3

Some business executives regard ratio analysis as the preserve of accountants. Nothing could be more wrong. Ratio analysis is an essential tool for the profit-driven manager. Ratios can either indicate the extent of the financial well-being of a business or give an early warning of an unsatisfactory trend.

Ratio analysis can be used to:

■ assess the current performance of a business, on a monthly basis

■ evaluate the acceptability of the budget proposed for the next financial year

■ compare the performance of subsidiaries and divisions within a group

■ compare performance with that achieved by competitors, on an annual basis.

The first step is to understand the definition of the various ratios used to evaluate business performance, and the significance of each one.

Return on investment

The key yardstick of financial performance within a business is the return on investment achieved, and it is usually measured annually.

The basic definition is simple:

% Return on investment =

$$\frac{\textbf{profit}}{\textbf{the amount invested to produce the profit}}$$

Sometimes ROI is used as an abbreviation instead of return of investment.

What happens in practice can be thoroughly confusing to non-accountants. Different definitions of profit and investment are used by different companies, and as a result different terms may be encountered such as 'return on capital employed' (ROCE) and 'return on operating assets' (ROA).

Fortunately, there is an easy way to cut through this confusion: ask one of the finance staff in your company to explain the definition they have adopted. Some accountants will debate the merits of their particular definition at length. When used to evaluate performance within a group or company, however, the most important features are that the definition adopted is:

■ easily understood by both managers and finance staff

■ used in a consistent way by each division and subsidiary.

because there is no consensus amongst qualified accountants in general of a correct definition of return on investment.

Nevertheless, it is helpful to know the alternative definitions most commonly used for profit and investment when used in connection with return on investment.

Profit is usually defined as either operating or trading profit, or profit before interest and tax, or as profit before tax.

Investment may be defined as:

- the average capital employed as shown on the balance sheet, ie. the fixed and current assets employed in the business minus all of the liabilities or

- the average operating assets employed, namely: fixed assets, plus current assets, less creditors due within one year, excluding bank overdrafts and other borrowings.

Clearly, the percentage return on investment figures calculated for a particular company may differ significantly depending upon the definitions chosen for profit and investment. For the purpose of comparison within a company, however, it is worth stressing that it is the changes and differences in the ratios which are of prime importance.

Freehold land and building valuation

In the balance sheet of a listed company, the valuation of freehold land and buildings will probably be updated at least every five years, in order to avoid a significant understatement of asset values. For a private company, if the freehold property is not needed as security for bank loans, the valuation in the balance sheet may be left at the original purchase cost of, say, over 20 years ago. The only reference to this undervaluation in the Annual Report may be an item in the Directors' Report stating that the current market value is greater than the figure shown in the balance sheet.

By calculating a return on investment on this undervalued freehold basis, however, the owners may be fooling themselves that the return on investment is satisfactory, when it is not. Consider the following example:

% Return on operating assets (ROA)

$$= \frac{\text{profit before interest and tax}}{\text{operating assets employed}}$$

$$= \text{say}, \frac{£264,000}{£1.2m}$$

= 22%, based on balance sheet valuation

If the value of the freehold property is understated by, say, £800,000, then on a current-valuation basis:

% Return on operating assets (ROA)

$$= \frac{£264,000}{£1.2m + £0.8m}$$

= 13.2%, based on current freehold valuation

Acceptable level of return on investment

It is a step forward to understand the calculation of return on investment, but this does not answer the important question 'What is an acceptable percentage return?'

Clearly the percentage return on investment should exceed:

- the percentage return achievable from a relatively risk-free investment such as a major building society, expressed grossed up for income tax at the standard rate – because otherwise a better return could be achieved simply by investing the money and receiving the interest

- the cost of overdraft interest – because otherwise the return achieved does not cover the borrowing cost of the investment.

In practice, however, an acceptable return on investment should be significantly higher than the above to provide an adequate reward for the risks involved and the management expertise required.

Many stockmarket-listed companies regard an acceptable return on operating assets, calculated using profit before interest and tax, to be a minimum of 20%. More importantly, however, these companies would regard 25% as a realistic goal to be achieved.

An analysis of return on investment

To manage the return on investment may seem to call for the ability to juggle simultaneously two completely different aspects of a business, profit and the funds invested. What is more, it may appear just as difficult to do as juggling, not two, but seven balls at once.

Fortunately, return on investment can be broken down into two separate and more easily manageable aspects of a business:

Return on investment

$$= \frac{\text{profit before tax and interest}}{\text{assets employed}}$$

$$= \frac{\text{profit before tax and interest}}{\text{sales turnover (or fee income)}}$$

x

$$\frac{\text{sales turnover}}{\text{assets employed}}$$

= % profit margin on sales

x

asset turnover

So the key to improving the return on investment is to increase:

- either the % profit margin on sales
- or the asset turnover
- or, better still, both of these.

To do either of these may seem almost as daunting as the apparent juggling needed to improve the return on investment. This is not so. Both the profit margin on sales and the asset turnover can be broken down into more easily manageable parts.

Profit margin on sales

The items which determine the % profit margin on sales are:

sales turnover or fee income

less

costs of sales

equals

gross profit

less

departmental overhead costs, including depreciation charges where these occur (eg. marketing, sales, research and development, production, distribution, finance, administration)

equals

profit before interest and tax.

Profit before interest and tax

So it becomes obvious that effective management and control of the % profit margin on sales requires attention to:

% gross profit achieved, ie. gross profit expressed as a percentage of sales turnover;

and

% departmental costs, ie. departmental costs expressed as a percentage of sales turnover.

The percentage profit before interest and tax on sales turnover tends to vary widely with the nature of the business. For construction companies it may be as low as between 2% and 4%. For food supermarkets and some wholesale businesses it may be between 3% and 5%. At the other extreme, some service companies may achieve more than 15%. Many businesses achieve less than 10% profit before interest and tax on sales turnover.

So every decimal point of percentage profit margin is important. For example, consider a business with an annual sales turnover of £10 million and the following budgeted costs for 1998:

1998 Budget	£m	
Sales turnover	10.00	100%
Cost of sales	3.88	38.8%
Gross profit	6.12	61.2%
Marketing	0.63	6.3%
Sales and customer service	2.37	23.7%
Distribution	0.90	9.0%
Development	0.93	9.3%
Finance and administration	0.47	4.7%
Profit before interest and tax	0.82	8.2%

During the year assume that the gross profit falls from 61.2% to 60.3%, ie. a decrease of only 0.9 percentage points. One response is to regard a gross profit of more than 60% to be a figure that many businesses would envy, and therefore to be acceptable. This would be totally unacceptable to the profit-driven manager. Assuming that departmental overhead costs remain the same percentage of turnover as budgeted, this means the profit margin will fall from 8.2% to 7.3%, ie. a similar decrease of 0.9 percentage of points. On a sales turnover of £10m, the profit before interest and tax will fall by £90,000 from £820,000 to £730,000.

Now consider a situation where:

■ the actual sales turnover falls to £9.5m compared with budgeted sales of £10m

■ the % cost of sales remains at the budgeted level of 38.8%

■ total overheads are allowed to remain at the budgeted amount of £5.3m.

Whereas the total overheads were budgeted to be 53% of sales turnover, if the overheads remain at £5.3m, these become 55.8% of the reduced sales turnover of £9.5m. So the profit margin will fall by a similar amount from 8.2% to 5.4%, because then overheads have increased by 2.8 percentage points. Profit before interest and tax will fall from £820,000 to £540,000.

So a clear message is evident. Whenever sales turnover falls, every effort must be made to reduce overhead levels as much as possible to partially offset the loss of profit, whilst avoiding lasting damage to the infrastructure of the business.

Asset turnover

The concept of managing asset turnover is likely to be less familiar to many managers than managing the profit margin on sales. It makes the point, however, that every pound of assets invested in the business must be made to work, or better still to 'sweat', to achieve the highest level of sales possible.

What does this mean in practical terms? Consider a hotel, with a ballroom that is used only in the evening for dinner dances and banquets. A relatively modest investment in movable partitions may allow the room to be used for conferences of various sizes during the day. The introduction of either a 'twilight shift' in the evenings or a seven-days-a-week 'continental shift' may allow for increased sales and asset turnover to be achieved from expensive production facilities. Equally, when new investment is being incurred to equip a new retail sales unit or to install costly production equipment, speed is essential. The aim must be to bring the facilities into use as soon as possible in order to increase asset turnover. Unused floor space, whether owned or rented, is costly. The action to be taken will depend upon how long the space is likely to remain unused. Possible action includes either subletting unused space on a short-term basis or relocating part of the business to allow a complete building to be let or sold.

Working capital must be used just as productively as investment in fixed assets. The main elements of working capital are stock and work-in-progress; debtors (cash owed to the business by customers) and creditors (cash owed by the business). Some managers believe that stock and work-in-progress levels, debtors and creditors are the responsibility of the finance function in the business. This is nonsense. Managers must exercise their accountability to manage these elements of working capital, with the assistance of finance staff.

Separate ratios need to be calculated for:

- Stock and work-in-progress
- debtors
- creditors.

Each one is defined and explained as follows.

Stock ratios

Stock ratios are usually expressed in one of two ways:

■ either the number of days of stock and work-in-progress held

■ or the number of times stock and work-in-progress is turned over annually.

The calculations are:

Stock turnover (days) =

$$\frac{\text{average stock and}}{\text{work-in-progress during year}}$$
$$\overline{\text{annual cost of sales}}$$

x

365
(number of days)

It may seem surprising that the annual cost of sales is used to calculate stock turnover rather than annual sales. The reason is simply to compare like with like, because stock values and cost of sales are calculated on the same basis.

Consider the following example:

	£m
Annual sales	10.00
Cost of sales	3.88
Gross profit	6.12
Stock and work-in-progress:	
at beginning of year	1.87
at end of year	2.21
Average stock and work-in-progress	2.04

$$\frac{\text{average stock and work-in-progress}}{\text{annual cost of sales}}$$

$$= \frac{£2.04 \text{ million}}{£3.88 \text{ million}} \text{ x } 365$$

$$= 192 \text{ days}$$

(Annual) stock turnover =

$$\frac{\text{annual cost of sales}}{\text{average stock and work-in-progress}}$$

$$= \frac{£3.88 \text{ million}}{£2.04 \text{ million}} = 1.9 \text{ times}$$

Of the two methods commonly used, the stock turnover in days is probably more meaningful for managers. If in the following year, the value of stock and work-in-progress were to increase from 192 days to, say, 199 days, it is obvious that it has taken an extra week to turn inventory into sales. The corresponding change in annual stock turnover from 1.9 times to 1.83 times is less revealing.

In a manufacturing company with a large investment in inventory, it may make sense to calculate separate ratios for:

■ raw materials

■ work-in-progress

■ finished goods ready for sale

in order to identify where corrective action is most needed.

Debtor ratio

On an annual basis, this is usually calculated by:

$$\text{Debtor ratio} = \frac{\text{debtors at year end}}{\text{annual sales}}$$

$$\times\,365$$

(number of debtor days)

On a monthly basis, this is often calculated on an equivalent number of days. For example, consider this calculation of the debtor ratio for June 1998:

Value of outstanding debtors at end of June		= £130,000
Invoiced sales	June	= £57,000
	May	= £63,000
	April	= £50,000

Outstanding debtors of £130,000 is equivalent to sales in:

June of	£57,000	= 30 days
May of	£63,000	= 30 days
April of	£10,000	= 6 days
		66 days

(pro rata to month of sales of £50,000)

Every business, regardless of size, should monitor the number of debtor days outstanding each month. An increase of only a single day during a month requires immediate corrective action.

Consider the impact of an increase in debtor days outstanding for a relatively small business with an annual sales turnover of £3.65m, ie. sales of £10,000 a calendar day. Assume that the average number of debtor days is allowed to increase by seven days throughout the financial year, ie. customers are allowed an extra week to pay their invoices. The effect is significant on both the bank overdraft and the amount of profit:

- the bank overdraft will increase by £70,000 (because an extra seven days sales, at £10,000 per day, will remain unpaid)

- the additional overdraft interest on additional borrowings of £70,000 for a year at, say, 9% interest will be over £6,000 a year.

In businesses with significant export sales, which may take considerably longer to be paid, there is a case for calculating each month the debtor days separately for:

- home sales
- export sales
- total sales.

Creditor ratio

On an annual basis, this is usually calculated by:

$$\textbf{Creditor ratio} =$$

$$\frac{\textbf{creditors at year end}}{\textbf{annual purchases}}$$

$$\textbf{x 365}$$

$$= \textbf{No. of creditor days}$$

On a monthly basis, this is often calculated on the basis of an equivalent number of days, in the same way as for debtors. By knowing the number of days of credit being taken from suppliers, it enables a manager to ensure that the policy of payment to suppliers is being adhered to, in overall terms.

Current ratio

A commonly used definition is:

Current ratio =

$$\frac{\textbf{current assets}}{\substack{\textbf{creditors due within a year,} \\ \textbf{excluding borrowings}}}$$

Current assets are primarily stocks, work-in-progress, debtors, cash-in-hand and any other liquid resources. The current assets represent the cash tied up in the business, but which is continually circulating. In a manufacturing company, raw materials are purchased, then pass through the work-in-progress stage during the production process, become finished goods, ie. stock for sale, are turned into debtors when the sale is invoiced and finally produce cash when the customer pays. The cycle starts again when some of the cash is used to purchase more raw materials.

Liquidity ratios

The survival of a business depends upon the ability to pay creditors acceptably soon enough. Liquidity ratios indicate the ability to pay creditors due within one year sufficiently quickly. There are two ratios:

■ current ratio

■ quick ratio.

Quick ratio

A commonly used definition is:

$$\text{Quick ratio} = \frac{\text{current assets, excluding stock and work-in-progress}}{\text{creditors due within one year}}$$

This means that the 'cash and near cash' resources, ie. debtors, cash-in-hand and any other liquid assets, are being compared with outstanding invoices which need to be paid.

If this ratio is less than 1.0, then the implications may be:

■ additional borrowings will be needed to pay creditors sufficiently quickly, or

■ extended credit will have to be taken, with the likelihood of court action for non-payment of invoices and the withholding of deliveries by suppliers

■ the business requires an injection of capital to finance the present scale of operations adequately.

Clearly, the current assets should comfortably exceed the value of creditors due for payment within a year to ensure that invoices can be paid sufficiently promptly. If the current assets were only to equal the creditors due within a year, then some increase in borrowings would probably be needed, simply because some of the current assets are tied up in stocks and work-in-progress, so will take longer to be turned into cash.

One rule of thumb which is used is that the current ratio of a healthy business should be at least 2.0, in order to provide an adequate safety margin to ensure that invoices can be paid sufficiently quickly. It has to be said, however, that many large and successful companies, with adequate unused borrowing facilities, operate on a current ratio much nearer to 1.0 than 2.0.

Nevertheless, some businesses do manage to survive for a surprisingly long time with a quick ratio significantly below 1.0. It has be to said, however, that the important word is 'survive'. Such a warning signal should not be ignored.

Gearing ratio

The gearing ratio shows the percentage of borrowed money in relation to the share-holders' funds in the company. A commonly used definition is:

Gearing ratio =

$$\frac{\textbf{net borrowings}}{\textbf{shareholders' funds}}$$

x 100%
(= percentage gearing)

Net borrowings are bank loans and over-drafts, minus cash-in-hand and other liquid resources.

Shareholders' funds are represented by the balance-sheet valuation of the shareholder's funds invested in the company. These are then issued as paid-up share capital, at nominal value, plus accumulated reserves. The reserves are the profit retained in the business since it was formed, plus any property-revaluation surplus and share-premium account where appropriate.

There are occasions when even companies listed on a stockmarket have a gearing ratio in excess of 100%. This means that lenders are providing more finance to operate the business than the shareholders. Indeed, there have been notable instances where listed companies have had a gearing ratio in the region of 250% – temporarily! This may have resulted from a major acquisition which involved a large amount of borrow-ing to pay for it. In these circumstances, however, it is likely that the Chairman's statement in the Annual Report will state what has already been done, and what more will be done, to reduce the level of gearing substantially. Indeed, it may be necessary to sell some businesses in order to reduce the gearing sufficiently quickly to an acceptable level.

The consequence of a high gearing ratio is a heavy burden of loan and overdraft interest charged to the profit-and-loss account. When the economic climate deteriorates, there may well be a compound effect on profit. Not only are trading profits likely to fall, but interest rates could increase as well.

One way of calculating the effect of gearing upon profit is to calculate the interest cover, which is commonly defined as:

$$\text{Interest cover} =$$

$$\frac{\text{trading profit or profit}}{\text{before interest and tax}}$$

$$\text{interest payable}$$

$$(\text{number of times})$$

A rule of thumb, and one which should not be ignored because the cost may be a loss of financial prudence, is that the interest cover should be at least 4.0, and preferably 5.0 or more, using the above definition.

Employee ratios

Some businesses use various employee ratios as a measure of productivity, especially during periods of rapid expansion when productivity may fall in the pursuit of growth. Ratios commonly used include:

- sales per employee – but this could be maintained or increased as a result of a higher 'bought-in material' or 'subcontracted' content of sales

- added value per employee – added value eliminates the possible distortion of any differences in the bought-in and subcontracted content by deducting these from sales

- profit before tax per employee – which can be highly revealing.

In professional partnerships, useful employee ratios include:

- average fee income per professional staff person

- average fee income per equity partner

- average profit before tax per equity partner.

For example, consider a professional partnership with:

Annual fee
income = £10.6m

Total fee earners = 50

Number of
equity partners = 10

Profit before tax = £2.4m

Average fee per
fee earner = £212,000 (£10.6m/50)

Average fee
income per
equity partner = £1,06,000 (£10.6m/10)

Average profit
before tax per
equity partner = £240,000 (£2.4m/10)

Another useful ratio to manage in a professional partnership is the professional staff support ratio, defined as:

Professional staff support ratio =

$$\frac{\textbf{total number of professional staff}}{\textbf{total number of other staff}}$$

To maintain profitability, any increase in this ratio must be adequately justified and not allowed to happen by accident or indulgence.

Indexation

When analysing trends in the performance of a company over five years or more, then even inflation of between 2% and 4% a year distorts the picture significantly. One method of analysis is to index the figures using a base of 100 for the first year; then to adjust subsequent years' figures using the movement in the appropriate index, such as the retail price index.

Using ratio analysis

Some managers want to know what is a 'good' or 'correct' figure for a particular ratio. This misses the essence of ratio analysis. For example, a 'nil' gearing ratio (indicating no borrowings at all) could be 'bad' rather than 'good'. It could reflect the fact that profitable opportunities have not been pursued because of an excessively conservative dislike of any borrowings.

As has been stated previously, some ratios differ widely according to the nature of the industry. The profit margins in the construction industry are likely to be dramatically lower than those of companies supplying luxury goods, as a generalisation.

Within a particular company, it is the trends which are of most importance. For example, ratio analysis reveals whether productivity and profitability are declining in the pursuit of rapid growth.

Comparisons with competitors

Ratio analysis provides the opportunity to compare or benchmark the performance of a company with that of competitors. Simply to obtain a copy of the published accounts of competitors and to calculate the ratios may produce some surprising contrasts, and some equally misleading figures because:

- profit may be calculated on a different basis

- balance sheets may be valued on a different basis.

Other significant differences in balance-sheet treatment exist. A company may have revalued property assets this year. A competitor may not have revalued property for four years. The accounting rules allow brand names which are purchased to be valued in the balance sheet. A small but growing number of companies now include a valuation of brand names purchased as part of a company acquisition in their balance sheets.

As a generalisation, an experienced accountant is needed to 'guestimate' the various adjustments needed to be made to published accounts for any worthwhile comparisons and conclusions to be made. Recognising this difficulty, in some trade associations the members submit their results in a standardised format to a major firm of chartered accountants in order for ratios to be circulated to the participants on an anonymous basis. Another source of useful information may be an inter-company ratio comparison available from a commercial publisher on selected business sectors.

Stockmarket ratio analysis

4

It would be understandable for a person working in a subsidiary or a division of a stockmarket-listed company to consider that stockmarket ratios are irrelevant to his or her job. The owner of a private company may take a similar view. Both would be equally wrong, for different reasons.

People working in stockmarket-listed companies need to know the yardsticks by which the performance of their company is judged, and the consequences for inadequate results, namely the real threat of being taken over, and the risk of substantial job losses.

For an owner of a private company, a knowledge of stockmarket ratios is needed to understand the performance required if it is decided to obtain a stockmarket listing, and to take a realistic view of the

amount an acquirer may pay to purchase the company.

At first sight, even the names of the various ratios seem complicated and daunting; gross dividend yield, dividend cover, earnings per share, price earnings ratio, market capitalisation and net asset backing per share sound like a foreign language. The reality is totally different. Once explained these ratios are simple to understand and calculate. Each ratio will be defined in turn, and then a worked example used to illustrate the calculation.

Gross dividend yield

The gross dividend yield is the return received by the shareholder by the receipt of a dividend, ignoring any deduction of income tax, calculated as a percentage of the current market price of the shares. The method of calculation is:

Gross dividend yield =

$$\frac{\textbf{gross annual dividend per share}}{\textbf{(before deduction of income tax)}}{\textbf{current market share price}}$$

This is a different calculation from that for the gross percentage dividend, which is:

Gross percentage dividend =

$$\frac{\textbf{gross annual dividend per share}}{\textbf{nominal value of share}}$$

So an understandable reaction would be, why bother with an extra calculation? The answer is simple. The percentage dividend allows comparison only with the dividend paid by the same company in previous years. The gross dividend yield allows a meaningful comparison to be made of the relative dividend income to be received from the shares of different companies.

Dividend cover

The dividend cover is the number of times the profits after tax earned for the ordinary shareholders exceed or 'cover' the gross dividend paid. The method of calculation is:

$$\text{Dividend cover} = \frac{\text{earnings}}{\text{gross dividend paid}}$$

The word 'earnings' is shorthand for the profits after tax earned for the ordinary shareholder in the parent company.

The dividend cover may be regarded as an indication of the safety margin by which the earnings exceed the gross dividend. If the dividend cover is 1.0, this means that the whole of the earnings, ie. profits after tax, has been used to pay the dividend to shareholders. If the dividend cover is less than 1.0, which sometimes happens, in effect the shareholders are being paid some of the capital value of their shares disguised as a dividend. This may be a conscious decision by the board, faced with a disappointing profit for the year, as a show of confidence by maintaining the same dividend payment in pence per share as was made in the previous year. The message behind this decision is 'Don't worry; the setback will not be repeated next year'. What it does mean, however, is that the company may have had to increase the overdraft to maintain the dividend payment, and so has to start the financial year facing an increased interest charge to the profit-and-loss account.

Earnings per share

The earnings per share is expressed in pence, and is the earnings for the year divided by the weighted average number of shares in issue during the year. The method of calculation is:

Earnings per share =

$$\frac{\textbf{earnings x 100}}{\textbf{weighted average number of issued shares}}$$

(pence per share)

The most important source of finance for any company is profit retained in the business, after paying corporation tax and an acceptable level of dividend to shareholders.

A stockmarket-listed company should aim to pay an adequate dividend yield and still be able to achieve a dividend cover greater than 2.0, ie. more profit should be left in the company to finance business development and growth than is paid to shareholders by dividend.

A key measure of profitability for a stockmarket-listed company is the growth in earnings per share, because it takes into account not merely trading profit from operations, but the effect of interest charges on profit and the overall level of corporation tax, so that the earnings are the total income earned from shareholders, and not just the amount of dividend paid, together with the ability to raise finance without issuing more ordinary shares.

Whenever additional shares are issued, for example:

- by a **rights issue** to existing shareholders to finance expansion

- to pay for the acquisition of another company, instead of using cash

- to executives under a share-option scheme

then the weighted average number of shares issued increases, and unless the earnings increase by a similar proportion, the earnings per share will be reduced. The expression often used to describe this situation is 'a dilution in the earnings per share'.

The aim of a stockmarket-listed company should be to maximise the growth in earnings per share throughout the medium and long-term, without a reduction of setback in any year.

The most successful companies of all listed on the stockmarket have achieved compound annual growth in earnings per share of more than 20% a year over a decade and longer.

Price-earnings ratio

Price-earnings ratios, often referred to as PE ratios, are published daily in *The Financial Times* for stockmarket-listed companies, along with the gross dividend yield, dividend cover and other information about the shares of each company. The method of calculation is what the name suggests:

Price-earnings ratio =

$$\frac{\text{stockmarket share price}}{\text{earnings per share}}$$

The stockmarket share price used is the one published in the financial newspapers at the close of business in the stock exchange for the previous evening.

On 3 May 1998 the average price-earnings ratio of a cross-section of several hundred companies was 22.2 This could be interpreted to mean that the share price of a typical company was 22.2 times the earnings per share achieved in the previous year.

As a generalisation, when the price-earnings ratio of a company is higher than the average for other companies in the same business sector, the stockmarket expects the company to achieve higher than average earnings per share in the foreseeable future to justify the above-average valuation of the shares.

In certain circumstances, the explanation may be quite different. For example, a takeover bid for the company may be widely expected, and the share price has already increased significantly in anticipation of the price to be offered by the bidder.

It must never be forgotten than the analysis of share prices, and especially the prediction of future changes, cannot be done simply by calculating the various ratios. If this was possible, making a fortune on the stockmarket would be easy. In practice, even the most experienced investment-fund managers make costly errors of judgement from time to time.

Market capitalisation

The market capitalisation of a stockmarket-listed company is simply the total value placed upon the shares of the company. It is calculated by:

Market capitalisation = number of issued shares x most recent share price

Of course, the market capitalisation does not indicate the price a takeover bidder would have to pay to acquire the company. Typically, even if a rival bidder does not make an increased bid, an offer of about 35% more than the share price when the offer was first anticipated may be needed for a successful bid. In a contested-bid situation, a successful bid may require to be at least 50% more than the previous price of the shares.

Net asset backing

The net asset backing is usually expressed in pence per share and is the balance sheet worth of each share. It is calculated by:

Net asset backing =

$$\frac{\textbf{shareholders' funds}}{\textbf{number of issued shares}}$$

(price per share)

The shareholders' funds consist of the issued share capital, calculated at the nominal value, plus reserves. In addition to retained profits, the reserves include the share premium account and any property revaluation where appropriate.

Some people find it surprising that the net asset backing per share shown by the audited balance sheet of a company may be significantly higher or lower than the present market price of the shares. Once again, the reason is simple. For most companies the prime determinants of the market share price are the most recent earning per share and the expected future growth. Balance sheet asset values tend to have a major influence on the share price only when there is a substantial proportion of the share price in the form of available cash within the company and readily saleable freehold properties.

For a profitable company which is not capital intensive, such as a successful advertising agency, the net asset backing per share may be only a small proportion of the market price of the shares. In contrast, consider a manufacturing company with poor profitability and high asset backing per share in the balance sheet. The likelihood is that the assets could not be turned into a corresponding amount of cash, even by liquidating the company. So the market share price will be depressed by the poor profitability, and may well be significantly lower than the net asset backing per share shown by the balance sheet.

Worked example

Consider the share information published by *The Financial Times* or in the City pages of other newspapers for a company on one particular day.

1998					Div.		Yield	
High	Low	Stock	Price	+ or −	net	Cover	Gross	P/E
595	425	XYZ 50p	558	-4	15.0	2.4	3.6	11.6

The information tells the reader that the:

- highest market share price to date in 1998 was 595p

- lowest market share price 425p

- nominal value of each share is 50p

- share price at the close of business last evening was 558p (the average of the buying and selling prices)

- (average) share price was 4p lower than the previous evening

- gross dividend yield in the previous year was 3.6%

- price-earnings ratio is 11.6 at the most recent share price of 558p.

The calculation of these stockmarket ratios for XYZ is shown overleaf.

$$\text{Gross dividend yield} = \frac{\text{gross dividend per share}}{\text{market share price}} = \frac{20.0p}{558p} = 3.6\%$$

$$\text{Dividend cover} = \frac{\text{earnings}}{\text{gross dividend paid}} = \frac{£412.0m}{£172.1m} = 2.4 \text{ times}$$

$$\text{Earnings per share} = \frac{\text{earnings}}{\text{weighted average number of issued shares}} = \frac{£412.0m}{860.6m} = 48p \text{ per share}$$

$$\text{Price earnings ratio} = \frac{\text{stockmarket share price}}{\text{earnings per share}} = \frac{558p}{48p} = 11.6$$

$$\text{Market capitalisation} = \text{number of shares issued at year end} \times \text{market share price} = 860.6m \times 558p = £4.8\ billion$$

$$\text{Net asset backing per share} = \frac{\text{shareholders' funds in balance sheet}}{\text{number of issued shares}} = \frac{£3,438m}{860.6m} = 399p\ per\ share$$

Comparative share performance

Occasionally, someone will ask 'What is a good PE ratio?', as if to imply that there is a universal and everlasting benchmark to aim for. This misses the point completely. Consider the sharp fall in share prices that occurred in October 1987 and affected the stockmarkets in many countries. The fall in share prices was more than 20% in many cases, which means that PE ratios fell by a similar percentage as a result, because the PE ratio is calculated by the most recent share price divided by the earnings per share. At any time, average PE ratios can differ significantly between the stockmarkets of different countries. Equally, the PE ratios for different types of business on the same stockmarket can vary widely.

The FT-Actuaries Share Indices table, published daily in *The Financial Times*, gives the PE ratios and gross dividend yields for a variety of business sectors. Some examples from the table (shown below) illustrate the wide differences which may occur:

	Gross dividend yield	PE ratios
Household Goods and Textiles	3.1	18.5
Electronical Equipment	3.0	25.7
Food Retailers	3.0	19.5
Paper, Packaging and Printing	4.2	13.3
FTSE All-Share index	2.8	22.2
covering 544 leading shares		

The most relevant comparisons to make for the shares of a particular company are with:

■ the sector average in the FT-Actuaries Share Indices table

■ broadly similar companies.

Consider the example of share performance (shown overleaf) of ABC plc, which operates in the Paper, Packaging and Print sector.

	Cover	Gross yield	PE ratio
ABC plc	2.9	4.6	9.4
Sector index	2.2	4.2	13.3
FTSE All-Share index	2.0	2.8	22.2
ANO plc	3.1	4.8	9.0
D and E plc	2.3	3.9	14.7
FGH plc	2.1	6.7	9.6

The observations and conclusions from the above figures are:

- the sector is rated substantially lower than the FTSE All-Share average, because the PE ratio for the sector is only 13.2, compared with the FTSE All-Share average of 22.2

- each of the above companies retains more than one half of its earnings, after paying dividends to shareholders, to finance business development and growth, because the dividend covers are greater than 2.0

- all of these companies pay a significantly higher dividend yield than the FTSE All-Share index, which gives shareholders a higher dividend income to compensate partially for the lower than average growth expected

- a lower than average PE ratio, implies that the market believes that future earnings per share growth will be below average, so all of these companies are expected to have significantly lower growth than the average of the 859 companies in the FTSE All-Share index

- a higher than average PE ratio, suggests a belief that future earnings per share growth will be above average, so D and E plc is expected to achieve higher growth then the average of companies in the sector

- ABC, ANO and FGH paid above average gross dividend yields in the previous year.

Share value in private companies

Owners of private companies sometimes have extravagant and quite unrealistic views about the worth of their business if it were to be sold. The use of PE ratios gives a broad indication of the possible price an acquirer may be prepared to pay.

Consider a privately owned building materials company. Assume the profits before tax in 1998 were £600,000, and an increase to £650,000 is forecast for 1999. The net assets of the business, taking into account the present value of the freehold property, is £2.4m. The owners believe the business is worth at least £5m.

Valuation of private companies using PE ratios is usually done on the assumption that a full rate of corporation tax, 31% in 1998/99, should be deducted from the profits before tax to calculate the earnings.

Actual profit before tax	**£600,000**
Less 31% corporation tax	**(£186,000)**
Earnings	**£414,000**

If on a particular date, the PE ratio of a sector is 14.0. The forecast profit growth for 1999 is roughly 'average', so one could assume the average PE ratio would be used by a takeover bidder. Wrong! The evidence is that buyers of private companies look for a discount on a comparable PE ratio for stockmarket-listed companies of at least 30%. This would suggest a PE ratio of about 9.8, calculated by deducting 30% from the sector average of 14.0. This suggests a valuation of 9.8 times the earnings of £414,000, of about £4m.

It must be stressed, however, that PE ratios give only a broad indication of the likely purchase price for a private company. Other factors will influence the purchase price to be obtained. Factors which tend to increase the purchase price include:

■ scarcity or rarity value, resulting from a shortage of attractive companies available to purchase in the sector

■ a market leader in a niche business

■ additional profit opportunities to be gained by the acquirer.

Factors which are likely to reduce the purchase price include:

■ undue dependence on one customer

■ low asset backing relative to the purchase price

■ particular reliance on the personal contribution of the present owners, which may be difficult to replace.

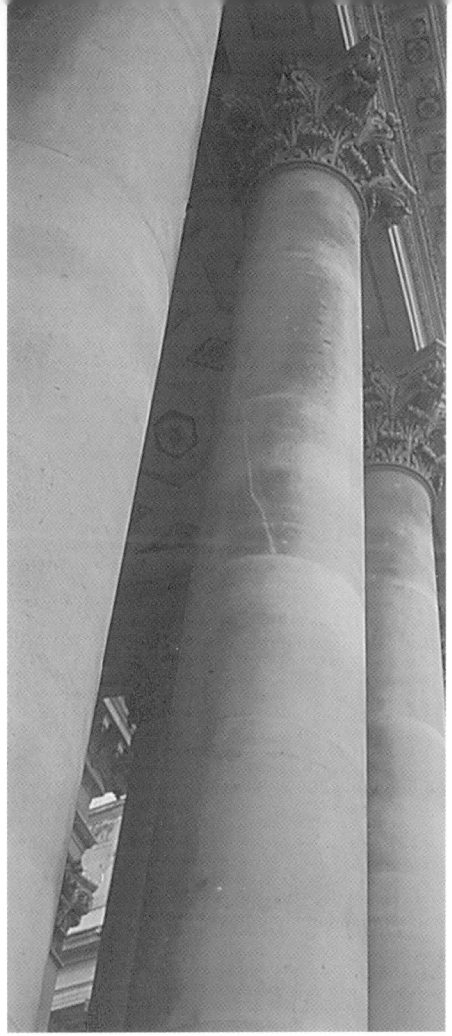

part **2**

Turning round
loss-making companies

The steps to recovery

5

An important way to achieve growth in profits is to turn round loss-making companies.

A surprising number of large companies have one or more subsidiaries making losses at any time. The number of private companies which fail is further ample proof of loss-making businesses. One response is a desire to sell the loss-making business, which is really an attempt to walk away from a situation which is both a problem and an opportunity. Even if a buyer is found, the purchase price is likely to be lower than net asset value. If a loss-making business is sold to the existing management interesting questions are raised. What will they do as owners of the business different from before? Why was this not done at the direction of the group previously? The opportunity is to turn the business into profit before considering selling it, because even if a sale makes sense, it will be easier to achieve and a much higher price should be obtained.

A new chief executive

It must be realised that the turn round of a loss-making business is unlikely to happen unless a new chief executive is appointed. Yet some groups tolerate losses from the same subsidiary for years before appointing a new chief executive to turn round the business. This is nothing less than costly procrastination. Strategic plans which are really a recipe for 'more of the same', without proposing drastic action, should be rejected. Equally, financial analysis alone will not produce the necessary results.

Almost certainly, the essential first step is to appoint a new chief executive with the authority to take the action needed to turn losses into acceptable profits as quickly as possible.

If there is an immediate cash-flow crisis threatening the survival of the business, then tackling this must be the main priority. Specific action which may be needed as a matter of urgency includes:

- meeting the bank and secured creditors to avoid receivership

- negotiating delayed payment of outstanding major trade creditors wherever possible, whilst reassuring people that effective corrective action is being taken quickly

- concentrating efforts on the collection of outstanding customer debts

- adopting a selective policy for paying creditors at least some of the money owed to them, to ensure continuity of essential supplies and services, and to avoid damaging legal action wherever possible.

Then there is a strong case for the newly appointed chief executive to make his or her presence felt. The seriousness of the

The impact of these measures may be modest in relation to the seriousness of the problems which exist. Nevertheless, they serve to make the point that the decks are being cleared in readiness for touch action to be taken where appropriate.

situation should be brought home by a variety of measures such as:

- terminating the employment of all temporary staff until further notice

  - if this could damage the business, someone is likely to scream loudly enough

- requiring personal approval of all overseas travel

  - the purpose of the visit must justify the expense involved and wherever appropriate the proposed visit schedule should be reviewed before approval is given

- suspending non-essential expense until further notice

  - for example, the employment of contractors to redecorate offices, the replacement of company cars, etc.

- delaying all non-essential capital expenditure for a period

- making all recruitment, including the replacing of existing staff, subject to chief executive approval

- eliminating any lavish entertainment or visible extravagance.

The main causes of the loss

The next step is to find out the main causes of the loss. The chief executive needs to talk with each member of the board and other members of the management team. Surprisingly often, the main causes quickly become apparent to someone newly appointed to the company. Possible causes may be:

- overhead costs are excessive in relation to sales volume

- the production cost of the service or product is too high compared with the market price

- there is overcapacity in the industry sector

- the marketing and selling efforts are ineffective and too costly

- product performance and customer benefits are no longer competitive

- poor product quality and reliability have undermined sales

- the need for expensive subcontract work to compensate for internal shortcomings.

Sales and marketing

The newly appointed chief executive needs to avoid becoming consumed by fire fighting day-to-day problems. A dispassionate and detailed examination of the business must be the main priority. A good place to start is by spending some time with sales staff. Accompanying people on sales visits to clients and prospective clients is often revealing. The shortcomings of the company are likely to become transparent. Problems such as unsatisfactory product performance, uncompetitive prices, unacceptable quality and reliability, late delivery and ineffective selling will be quickly exposed.

Visits with sales staff will expose any shortcomings of the sales-support team. So it makes sense to examine sales-support departments next.

Only then should attention be focused on marketing activities. The contribution of marketing to the business needs to be measured. The level of expense needs to be assessed critically. It is all too easy for marketing activity to be confused with marketing effectiveness. In an actual case, the marketing staff was cut from 17 people to eight. Afterwards, it was generally accepted throughout the business that the contribution of marketing had increased substantially as a result of better direction, despite operating with a much smaller staff.

Urgent financial analysis should be carried out to confirm some of the main causes of the losses. Aspects which need to be assessed include:

- the marginal profit percentage produced by each product or service group

- major customer profitability

- the break-even point of the business based upon existing overhead levels

- the maximum affordable fixed overhead costs to break-even on present sales volume and prices.

Time does not allow for precise financial analysis to be done. The need is for sufficiently accurate information to be produced quickly.

Production and delivery

The production and delivery of the products or services supplied to customers should come under scrutiny next. Questions which need to be answered include:

- What scope is there to apply value-engineering techniques to the specification of products or services?

- What is the speed of delivery and the reliability of delivery promises?

- How much business is lost by late delivery or part delivery?

- What bottlenecks exist and how can these be overcome?

- What needs to be done to improve product or service quality and reliability?

- What can be done to reduce costs significantly?

- What outsourcing opportunities should be evaluated?

- What additional expenditure would produce an attractive financial return quickly?

Head office

The head office needs critical examination. The role and contribution of head office requires careful definition. The minimum possible number of staff needed should be assessed. Wherever possible, operating businesses should be responsible for providing the full range of services needed in order to be managed as autonomous units.

Administration costs should be attacked. Satisfactory answers are needed to questions such as:

- What would happen if the work was left undone?

- Why is it done so often?

- Why is it done in such an expensive way?

- If it really needs to be done, how could it be handled at much lower cost?

Research and development

Research and development can prove a difficult area to tackle. The chief executive appointed may lack technical knowledge compared to senior development staff. This need not necessarily be a disadvantage. Questions to be answered which cut through the technical complexities include:

- How does the level of research and development expenditure compare with leading competitors?

- What percentage of total research and development costs are spent upon:

  - pure research?

  - new product development?

  - further development of existing products?

- What percentage of current sales is represented by new products or services introduced during the last five years?

- What is the percentage of sales from new products and services contributed by:

  - internal research and development?

  - licensing, royalty or distribution agreements?

  - joint venture co-operation?

- How are research and development projects evaluated commercially and financially before work is commenced?

- Is there adequate liaison between research and development, marketing and production staff?

- Are effective project-management and cost-control techniques used?

- What new projects should be authorised or evaluated to meet the market needs?

Rationalisation

Now the time has come to address the need for rationalisation of the business and a reduction in staff levels and overhead costs in order to achieve a break-even situation quickly. The range of products and services offered may need drastic pruning. A list of products and services in descending order of the amount of either marginal profit or gross profit produced by each one may be revealing. In an actual example, out of nearly 500 products six accounted for more than 80% of the total marginal profit produced. Substantial reduction of the product range was achieved, without any significant adverse customer reaction.

Staff will have realised that redundancies will happen, without having been told. The sooner the redundancies are announced, the sooner the uncertainty is ended. In the meantime, the staff most likely to leave are the more talented people, who will find it easier to get other jobs, which is another reason for speed.

The overall number of people to be made redundant needs to be decided first, compatible with maintaining a viable infrastructure within the business and leaving an affordable level of overhead costs. Any suggestion of rateable cuts in each department must be rejected. The chief executive should agree with the manager of each department the number of redundancies required. Disproportionately large cuts may be required at head office and in administration departments. It is even possible that some modest recruitment may be necessary at the sharp end of the business, such as in direct sales staff or installation engineers.

Each manager should be required to propose a list showing the required redundancies. The chief executive should review each list, to be satisfied that an objective selection has been made. Then people need to be informed. This should be done face-to-face, and handled with understanding, generosity and compassion. Trade unions will need to be notified where appropriate.

If possible, help should be given to assist people to obtain other jobs. There is no ideal time to announce redundancies, but a Friday afternoon makes sense. This means that only those people still employed with the company will return to work on the following Monday morning. Disaffected people who have been made redundant must not be allowed to linger on.

It is important that all of the redundancies should be announced at one time.

Morale will be affected, but much worse so if people are left to speculate when the next round of redundancies will be announced. The sooner that the business needs to start recruiting people again, the better it is for morale.

At this stage, the reduced level of fixed costs will be known by the chief executive and the overall percentage marginal profit presently achieved. So it is easy to calculate the annual sales value required to break-even. This should be translated into a monthly sales target needed to break-even, and the management team should collectively be committed to the goal of the first month in which the break-even sales value will be exceeded and so eliminate the losses.

Financial recovery

The next step should be to involve the board or executive committee in setting revised and demanding sales and profit forecasts for the remainder of the current year. The opportunity should be taken to improve monthly management information in order to provide people with the information needed to manage the business effectively.

Rigorous budget preparation is needed for the next financial year.

People must realise that the elimination of losses is not enough; it is only the first and relatively easy stage on the road to financial recovery.

The goal must be to achieve an acceptable return on the operating assets employed as quickly as possible.

In a turn-round situation, an important part of the budget should be a number of profit-improvement projects, with each one:

- designed to achieve rapid profit improvement
- having a member of the board accountable for timely and successful completion.

Once the initial surgery has been carried out and profit-improvement projects initiated, it is time to get down to business development in earnest. A fundamental issue needs to be addressed. Now that the initial turn-round work has been done, should the chief executive continue? Or be replaced by someone better suited to carry out the business-development work? This may seem a surprising question to raise. It may well be, however, that the turn-round person is not ideally suited to stay on through the medium term to achieve the business development needed.

The evidence available shows that surgery and short-term profit-improvement action are likely to eliminate losses but that major new initiatives are needed to achieve an acceptable financial return. There is no substitute for:

- creating a vision statement
- adopting the quantum leap approach
- identifying and evaluating strategic options
- establishing an effective organisation structure
- setting up major business-development projects.

part

How to boost profits this year

Budgets and budgeting control

6

Budgeting in some large groups of companies has become nothing more than a time-consuming management game, despite the fact that the procedures used represent what may be described as 'best practice'. Some private companies have prospered for many years without even any rudimentary budgeting. So, why bother to budget?

Sound budgets, prompt monthly reporting of actual results, and a regularly updated forecast of the results expected for the financial year are the essential foundations of financial management and control.

Basic issues

First-class procedures are not sufficient to ensure effective budgeting and budgetary control.

Appropriate management attitudes are essential. These require two basic issues to be addressed:

1 What level of achievement should the budget reflect?

2 Who is responsible for achieving budgeted performance?

Even within a group of companies, the level of achievement reflected in budgets may vary widely. A subsidiary company may set a budget that is an optimistic target, with little real commitment to achieving it. At the other extreme, another subsidiary may set a budget based upon the minimum results likely to be achieved, even if adverse circumstances arise unexpectedly. Both of these are equally unacceptable. The budgeted level of performance should be demanding, but achievable by committed and co-ordinated management action.

It is not enough for the managing director, general manager, or a regional manager in charge of a separate business to be committed to the achievement of the budgeted profit. Nothing less than the collective cabinet commitment of the person in charge and each member of the team reporting directly to him or her is acceptable. Otherwise, people may adopt the parochial view that their only responsibility and concern is to achieve the sales or control the costs in line with their departmental budget. This would be nonsense, and must not be allowed to happen. For example, if the gross profit from sales falls below budget then every effort must be made to offset this by appropriate cost reduction throughout the business.

Budget assumptions

The assumptions on which the budget is to be constructed should be agreed by the executive team, and written down at the outset, otherwise different departments may make inconsistent assumptions. Even if this is avoided, it is difficult for a higher level of management to review the proposed budget objectively and to justify and changes required. Assumptions which need to be made and written down include:

- price increases for existing products and services
  - the proposed percentage increase and date to be implemented for each product or service group
- the date for the launch of each new product or service
- the dates planned for other events which will affect the budget such as:
  - new branch or store openings
  - relocation of premises
  - the appointment of additional distributors

- expected salary increases
- cost inflation for the various categories of expenditure
- currency exchange rates and commodity price movements, where appropriate
- the recruitment of additional staff
- major items of discretionary expenses within departmental budgets, such as advertising or research and development
- substantial capital expenditure projects
- impact of anticipated legislation and other external factors such as:
  - higher national insurance contributions
  - additional costs arising from recently announced EC requirements on food packaging.

Co-ordination

Most businesses are organised into numerous separate departments and functions.

If detailed budgets are prepared by each department and then simply aggregated into an overall budget for the business, the resulting profit and cash flow may be unacceptable. Co-ordination at an early stage is needed to ensure this does not happen.

One could argue that the widespread use of personal computers and spreadsheet programs has made budget revisions quick and easy to carry out. This is so, but overlooks the demotivating effect of being instructed to revise a detailed budget. People need to feel it is their budget, if they are to be totally committed to achieving it.

An effective way to achieve the co-ordination is by the executive directors of the business collectively preparing and agreeing an acceptable outline budget before the preparation of detailed departmental budgets is started.

The outline budget needs to be no more than an outline profit-and-loss and cash-flow budget for the year. It means, however, that each director will know what departmental budget will be acceptable from the outset.

Sales budget

Ideally, the sales budget will be prepared and the implications for other departments discussed with them, before they need to start preparing their detailed budgets. Otherwise, departments such as purchasing, production, order processing and physical distribution will have to base their budgets upon a 'guestimate' of the volume and mix of sales to be budgeted.

Every effort must be made to budget sales as accurately as possible, despite the uncertainties involved. Any variance between budgeted and actual sales is likely to have a disproportionately greater effect on budgeted profit and cash flow.

The pareto effect can be used to advantage. This probably means that 20% of the total number of customers may account for at least 80% of total sales value. Alternatively, where sales are made direct to the individual consumer, such as in retail stores, 20% of the total number of product lines may well represent a substantial proportion of the total sales value. For those 20% of customers or products, every effort must be made to assess budgeted sales individually. Sales value should not merely be estimated as a total amount, but should be calculated from the number of units to be sold and the sales prices to be obtained. Up-to-date facts on recent current orders from these customers are important background for predicting future changes in demand.

Some service businesses, such as patent agents or plumbers, may argue correctly that for a large part of their fee income for the budget year it is difficult to predict even the identity of their clients accurately and impossible to budget for the fee income from individual clients. Nevertheless, there are ways around these problems.

Records will show the number of hours invoiced by each professional staff member during the preceding 12 months. From this, surprisingly accurate estimates can be made for the invoiced hours to be charged during the budget year. Together with the budgeted number of fee earners to be employed and the hourly fee rates to be charged, the total fee income can usually be budgeted with surprising accuracy.

Overhead costs

The annual budgeting exercise provides an opportunity not merely to budget departmental costs for the coming year but also to challenge the existence, size and methods of each department. Unfortunately, not enough companies seize the opportunity available.

It may sound like a recipe for anarchy, but it is not. The technique is known as zero-based budgeting and variations of it have been used for many years by some companies. In essence, it means adopting a 'blank-piece-of-paper approach' by considering how the need would best be served if the department did not exist at all. For example, perhaps physical distribution of goods would be outsourced completely rather than be provided by company-owned vehicles with a large number of staff employed. Or at least vehicles would be leased, instead of owned.

In some large companies, zero-based budgeting techniques have been introduced and brought no worthwhile benefits, the reason being that managers were required to fill in many more standard spreadsheets. The idea of challenging the *status quo* was lost. Instead, people used the standard spreadsheets to justify not changing the present situation. It is worth stressing again that the real benefits to be gained from zero-based budgeting arise from thinking about and challenging existing methods and standards, not from a cynical approach of the need to fill in yet more standard spreadsheets.

Staff salaries, and the costs which inevitably occur as a result of employing staff, are a major part of most overhead-cost budgets.

It is quite inadequate simply to budget a lump sum for staff costs; a detailed analysis needs to be done. Headcount numbers for each department should be budgeted month by month. Where additional staff are to be recruited during the budget year, each appointment should be specified in the following detail:

- job title
- salary and benefits
- date when employment will commence
- estimated capital expenditure required, eg. company car, personal computer
- method and cost of recruitment.

It is unacceptably sloppy to budget for additional staff on the naive assumption that each person will join on the first day of the financial year.

When departmental overhead budgets are reviewed by higher-level management, the list of additional staff proposed should be challenged critically. The need to terminate staff when sales fall significantly below budgeted levels is costly, painful, time-consuming and generally demotivating across the business. The most effective way to avoid the problem is to take a hard-nosed approach to any excessive or premature staff recruitment proposed in a departmental budget.

Sizeable round sums for discretionary items such as trade exhibitions or press advertising should not be accepted. If a sum of, say, £150,000 is included in the budget, sufficient analysis must be provided, for example the exhibitions to be attended and the costs of each one. Press advertising should be detailed by the number of adverts to be placed in each newspaper at an average cost per insertion.

Lump sums are equally unacceptable for items such as patent costs and overseas travel. The forecast cost for the current year, plus adjustments to reflect increased sales volumes and anticipated cost inflation is unsatisfactory as a basis for budgeting costs such as these. Patent costs need to be budgeted in terms of the number of applications to be made in each country, multiplied by the average costs expected in each country. Overseas travel needs to be budgeted on an estimated basis, based on who will need to travel to which countries for how long.

Capital expenditure

Once again detail is required; a lump sum approach is unacceptable.

Individual projects should be listed, and the total capital expenditure costs estimated for each one. Associated revenue costs connected with a project should be estimated, so that these are not omitted from the appropriate overhead-cost budget, for example the cost of additional software to be purchased with each personal computer. Equipment which needs to be replaced merely to continue in business must not be overlooked, for example the need for the existing telephone switchboard to be replaced by a larger one because the volume of calls can no longer be handled adequately.

The month in which each piece of capital expenditure will be invoiced by the supplier needs to be set out as part of the detailed budget. This may be thought excessive detail, but it is not. The combination of the proposed timing of capital expenditure and the differing working-capital needs of the business during the year may exceed the borrowing facilities of the company. The only way to avoid this is to plan the capital expenditure on a month-by-month basis.

Every manager needs to realise that the inclusion of a particular project in an approved capital-expenditure budget does not in any way automatically authorise the expenditure.

Most companies rightly require a detailed commercial and financial justification to be presented and approved for all capital projects over a certain value. Equally, it is nonsense for a manager to be told during the budget year that a project will not be authorised because it was not itemised in the budget. Surely, if circumstances or priorities have changed, the manager should be allowed the proposed project provided that other capital expenditure items of a similar value are deleted.

The cash budget

For many types of business, cash is more difficult to budget accurately than profit. Even if actual sales are exactly in line with budget each month, there is no guarantee that customers will pay their invoices within the time allowed in the budget. Despite the inevitable inaccuracy, however, the most important budget of all is the cash budget. What is more, an annual cash budget is totally inadequate without additional detail. The cash budget must be calculated month by month, because there may be wide fluctuations during the year in the size of the overdraft required.

Every item of cash must be included such as:

- cash received from customers
    - based upon the budgeted period time to be allowed for payment by customers
- interest payable or receivable
- payments to trade creditors
    - based upon a budgeted payment period from receipt of suppliers' invoices
- salaries and associated employment costs, such as pension and national insurance contributions
- capital expenditure, identified on a month-by-month basis.

Quarterly, six-monthly and annual outgoings need to be included, such as:

- rental and lease payments
- rates
- interim and final dividends
- advance corporation tax
- corporation tax
- insurance premiums
- bonus payments.

Monthly budget phasing

Obviously, to produce a monthly cash budget means that annual sales need to be budgeted on a month-by-month basis as well as operational costs and capital expenditure. This monthly analysis is often referred to as calendarising or phasing the budget.

Sales need to be calendarised on a monthly basis as accurately as possible. Most business have seasonal fluctuations in sales, caused by a variety of factors. These must be taken into account.

Fortunately, history may provide a reliable guide for monthly budget phasing sales. A useful exercise is to calculate the percentage of annual sales which took place in each month of the previous three years. The pattern may be sufficiently similar to provide a reliable guide for the budget year.

Equally, the budgeted annual profit must be phased monthly in order to know whether or not the business is on course to achieve the budgeted profit throughout the year. Some businesses phase the budgeted profit only quarter by quarter, but this does not provide a sufficiently early warning of a profit shortfall.

Effective monthly reporting

Monthly reporting needs to be prompt. Information which is sufficiently accurate, but includes some estimated figures, should be produced within one or two weeks of the end of each monthly or four weekly accounting period. After all, in the following month any estimates which were made can be adjusted to the actual figures. Some companies take three or four weeks to produce monthly results which is unacceptable.

Sales figures should be circulated daily, weekly or monthly because these give an indication of likely performance against the budgeted profit. Even earlier indications of subsequent profit performance can be obtained in some businesses. For example, in an estate-agency business with numerous branches it may be useful to monitor each week the number and value of:

- properties on which sale instructions have been received, with separate figures either on a sole – or joint-agency basis

- contracts which have been exchanged for the sale of properties

- mortgage applications made on behalf of purchasers.

Although it may take several months from receiving an instruction to sell a property to a legally completed sale, the number of new instructions received each week is likely to provide a reliable guide to trends in future income.

With the widespread use of personal computers, managers tend to be inundated with figures and print-outs, but often lack sufficient useful information for management action. For example, a schedule of all debtors requires time to be spent to identify those customers where further action is needed to collect outstanding debts. To compound matters, some debtor listings include all customers who have made a purchase during a financial year, even if they do not owe any money at present.

Summary information which is particularly useful for management action includes:

- a list of all customers with a debt outstanding for either 60 or 90 days, perhaps listed in decreasing order of size to focus immediately on the largest amounts

- a list of any customers which have been allowed to exceed their authorised credit limit.

Computer-produced graphics are a useful way of displaying a lot of data effectively. The capability to produce diagrams such as bar charts, pie charts and graphs is widely available with personal computers. Sadly, not enough accountants who are responsible for producing monthly reports in companies make sufficient use of the facility. If necessary, a manager should request the accountant to present information using graphics.

A set of monthly reports needs to be accompanied by a narrative to comment upon and to explain significant items. Without a narrative, the value of the figures is much reduced. When the monthly reports are to be reviewed at a board or management committee meeting, it is important that the reports and narrative are circulated in sufficient time for participants to have considered them before the meeting. Otherwise, not only is time likely to be wasted in the meeting but the discussion may well be unduly superficial too.

Monthly reporting should not be restricted to financial statements produced by the finance department. The information presented should be what is needed for the effective management of the business, and may include the value, or number of:

- proposals or tenders submitted
- orders received
- employee numbers compared with budget
- sales lost through unavailability of stock.

Financial year forecasts

Once a budget has been authorised, any revision should be firmly resisted, even if the cause was either unforeseen or completely outside the control of the business.

For example, an unexpected supplementary budget by the government which increases the national insurance contributions payable by employers. Managers will always be keen to seek a revision which reduces the budgeted profit, but a request for an increase is unheard of. As soon as a budgeted profit is reduced, this immediately becomes an acceptable standard of performance. The original budget is quickly forgotten.

This must not be allowed to happen. For a stockmarket-listed company to explain a disappointing profit performance in terms of some subsidiaries failing to achieve budget would be unthinkable. It would be nothing less than an unacceptable and naive excuse. The management team must focus on the action to be taken to achieve the budgeted profit despite unforeseen setbacks.

Situations arise where during the early months of the year, the actual profit is in line with budget but events have already occurred which will adversely affect the remainder of the year. Examples include a reduction in the level of enquiries or orders received, an adverse change in currency-exchange rates and bank interest levels, or an unexpected increase in raw-material costs.

Forecasts of profit and cash flow for the full financial year should be updated regularly to quantify any shortfall expected. The year-end forecasts should be updated at least quarterly. Better still, the forecast should be reviewed monthly and amended whenever necessary. Whilst the forecast will be prepared by the finance staff, it should be based upon discussions with the management team responsible for achieving it. Also, when a revised forecast is produced, it should be accompanied by a concise narrative to explain the changes and the reasons for them. The existence of a year-end forecast enables the board or management committee meeting to concentrate on what further action is to be taken to improve the forecast profit, rather than merely review the result for the previous month.

Monthly report summary

In some large companies, each subsidiary is required to produce a monthly report of anything from 10 to 30 detailed schedules. Quite often most of this information is ignored by the senior executives within the subsidiary. Worse still, despite the mass of detailed figures presented, there may be no summary of key information.

The first page of a monthly reporting package should be a Monthly Report Summary. This should provide the key information about the business at a glance.

The content of the summary should reflect what is particularly relevant to a given type of business. For an illustration, see overleaf.

Monthly report summary

	Month	Better (worse than budget)	Year to date	Better (worse than budget)	Full year forecast	Better (worse than budget)
Sales	357	(23)	1,403	37	4,350	(150)
Gross profit	173	(17)	707	19	2,250	(50)
Total overhead	162	(5)	546	7	1,830	(13)
Bank interest	5	(1)	22	(2)	70	(8)
Profit before tax	6	(23)	139	24	350	(71)

	Last month		This month		Year end	
Bank overdraft	396	14	412	(12)	520	(70)
Debtor days	48	(3)	47	(2)	45	–
Creditor days	63	(3)	61	(1)	60	–
Work-in-progress	547	(47)	560	(55)	630	(90)
Total staff	51	(1)	47	1	52	2

£ million

Sales

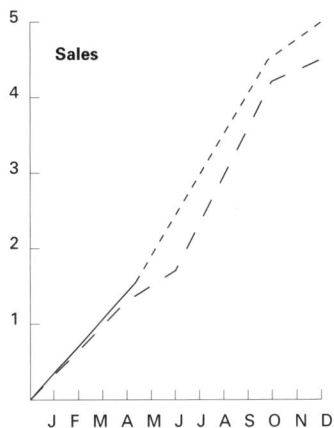

£ thousand

Bank overdraft

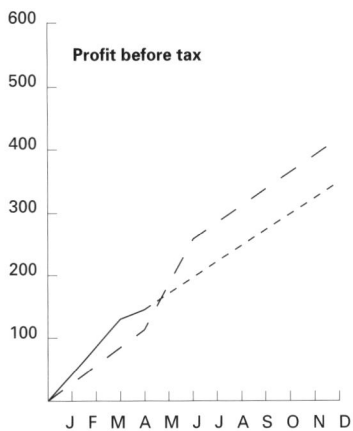

£ thousand

Profit before tax

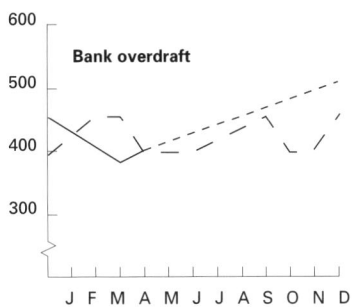

Key:

actual ——————

forcast – – – – – – – ·

budget — — — —

Cash management

A receiver, or liquidator, is appointed when creditors are not paid sufficiently promptly. At the time, the business may have made a small profit in the current month or the owners may feel confident that losses will be turned into profits during the next few months. The business may be expanding.

All of this counts for nothing if creditors cannot be paid sufficiently quickly. Indeed, one of the causes of the problem may be that the business has been expanding too rapidly in relation to the amount of finance available.

It would be entirely wrong to give the impression, however, that cash management is needed only when a business might be facing receivership.

Effective cash management is so important that every business should practise it 365 days a year, and to emphasise the point, 366 days each leap year.

The profit-driven manager knows that cash management is essential to optimise profit. Otherwise the amount of bank interest payable will be unnecessarily large. The finance staff do not manage the business, and neither do they manage cash. In both cases, they merely assist their colleagues in the management team. Cash management is a key executive task.

The foundation for effective cash management is a detailed cash-flow budget, calendarised month by month, as described already. Before each month commences, however, it may be appropriate to make an updated daily or weekly forecast in order to keep a tighter rein on cash. The other essential ingredients of cash management include:

- ensuring that customers pay promptly
- planning and controlling the amount of money tied up in stock and work-in-progress
- paying creditors sufficiently quickly to avoid either commercial disadvantage or financial penalty
- making sure that the level of overhead costs is affordable
- ensuring that adequate finance and bank overdraft facilities are available
- monitoring performance against the cash-flow budget regularly
- maintaining a dialogue with the bank.

In addition, a prudent and rigorous approach is needed for capital expenditure decisions. This will be covered in chapter eight.

Debtor management

Debtor management is the entire process of obtaining prompt payment by customers. Some people imagine that all it involves is sending out invoices and writing reminder letters to customers who do not pay sufficiently quickly. If only it was that simple, but nothing could be further from reality. Some of the main elements of debtor management are:

Deposit with order

Whenever a custom-made product or service is supplied, a policy requiring a minimum deposit with the order should be considered. Such a policy should definitely be adopted, unless valid reasons exist which would damage the business. It is not necessarily a valid argument that none of your competitors has a similar policy. Many companies and professional partnerships have found a surprising willingness by customers or clients to make an initial payment, especially when the amount of work involved is explained to them.

Interim invoicing

Many service businesses overlook valid opportunities for interim invoicing. An awful example concerned a firm of solicitors experiencing an excessively high overdraft level, and under considerable pressure from the bank manager to reduce it. Interim invoicing was almost non-existent. There was one major case being handled by the senior partner, and after almost six years no interim invoice had been sent. In these circumstances, the client is likely to be shocked by the size of the invoice and to have forgotten the amount of work involved and even the benefits received.

Interim invoicing should be agreed at the outset as a matter of routine. The aim should be to invoice the client as soon as each stage is completed.

Prompt invoicing

When goods are supplied to a customer, the use of multi-part stationery automatically produces the invoice at the same time as the items are despatched. Substantial delay may occur, however, before a service is invoiced.

Consider a car-maintenance service performed by a garage. There are still some garages which apologise for not providing an invoice when the car is collected, yes apologise, because they are too busy. The invoice will be posted in a few days' time. Contrast this with a garage with effective cash management. The customer may well be expected to pay for the work before collecting the car, unless it is to be paid by a previously arranged monthly company account. If the car is to be collected after the garage has closed, the customer will be asked to provide: either a signed cheque made out to the garage, for them to complete when the cost is known; or a credit card slip to be signed when the car is delivered, so that the cost can be entered by the garage later.

Companies and firms providing a service carried out by professional staff tend to delay sending out invoices unnecessarily. Often the reason is simple, and easily remedied. The invoice needs to be written by the person providing the service, who regards it as an administrative chore which can be put off. The remedy is that each professional staff person should have a demanding monthly budget of invoiced fees to achieve.

Creditworthiness

Invoicing promptly is important, but is assumes that the customer has the ability and intention to pay. The potential problems are when supplying some private companies and individuals.

The credit status of private companies should be checked. Simply to request references from two other suppliers may be inadequate. The customer may pay these two accounts promptly purely to have references available. Equally, a bank reference may not reveal sufficient information about the customer. Also, beware of the customer placing two or three small orders and paying them promptly, only to follow these with a large order without the ability or intention to pay. An up-to-date credit-status report on a company can be purchased for a few pounds. Obviously, credit-status checks should be used selectively, rather than as a matter of routine, as by some businesses. The message is clear, however, – if in any doubt, obtain a credit-status report.

It is difficult to check the creditworthiness of an individual. Outward appearance may create the impression of wealth, but be nothing more than deliberate deceit. Cash with order should be requested or at least a worthwhile initial payment. A definite limit should be set for the maximum amount of credit to be allowed, and this should be strictly adhered to.

Credit limits

For many businesses, it makes sense to set a credit limit for each corporate customer, to establish the maximum credit which will be allowed at any time. Whenever the limit would be exceeded by supplying another order received, the appropriate manager should be alerted. One phone call requesting payment of some of the existing debt before the next order is completed may produce a cheque immediately.

Eliminating excuses

Some customers make a successful habit of waiting until they are pressed for payment to point out the omission of basic information on the invoice, such as:

- customer order number
- supplier's VAT number
- delivery address.

They will point out that until this information is provided, the invoice cannot even be accepted. Once again, the remedy is simple.

Ensure that all the relevant order information, including the terms of payment, is clearly and accurately stated on the invoice.

Prompt-payment discount

In theory, a discount on the invoiced price which ensures prompt payment seems like a good idea. The reality may be quite different. Two issues need to be considered – the cost and the benefit.

Some companies offer a 2.5% discount for payment within seven or ten days of the date of the invoice. If as a result a customer pays the invoice two months earlier than without such an incentive, then this is equivalent to an annualised cost of 15% to the supplier. This is because a 2.5% cost for receiving payment two months earlier must be multiplied by six to arrive at the annualised cost. When compared with the alternative cost of having a correspondingly large overdraft, this may appear reasonable in certain circumstances. If as a result of a 2.5% prompt-payment discount, however, the customer pays only a month earlier, then the annualised cost to the supplier is 30%, which is expensive.

Worse still, some large customers may pay their invoices after, say, a month and still automatically deduct the prompt-payment discount. Faced with this situation, some sales managers accept it rather than risk upsetting an important customer. This is far removed from effective cash management.

Requesting payment

On the day that payment becomes due, a request for payment should be made. A standard letter, produced by computer on flimsy paper with poor print quality and addressed simply to the Accounts Department, is almost certain to have no effect. It is likely to be regarded as junk mail and consigned immediately to the wastepaper bin.

When an order is accepted, the name, position and address of the person who will authorise payment should be established. In a multi-national company, invoices may need to be sent to a regional or head office located in another country.

The request for payment should be addressed to the correct individual. It should ask that any reason why payment has not been made should be notified immediately. E-mail or facsimile should be used to avoid delay.

Telephone follow-up

If payment has not been received seven days from the first request for payment, a telephone call should be made to the person responsible for authorising payment. If the response is unsatisfactory, the person who placed the order should be telephoned and asked to obtain payment without further delay. If any queries, reasons or excuses are raised to justify non-payment, these must be answered or dealt with immediately. Sometimes two or three weeks will be taken to answer a query, which is effectively granting extended credit to the customer as a result of administrative incompetence.

Further action

If payment is not forthcoming, further action should be taken within a matter of days. Delay or, more accurately, procrastination is likely to reduce significantly the chances of receiving payment at all. According to the amount and country concerned, either a debt-collecting agency or a solicitor should be instructed.

Stock and work-in-progress management

The cost of holding raw materials, production work-in-progress and finished goods ready for sale is alarmingly high. Various studies carried out by major companies have demonstrated that the annual cost of holding stock is between 25% and 40% of the value of stock. In other words, every £1m of inventory costs between £250,000 and £400,000 a year to hold in stock.

At first sight, these figures seem difficult to believe. When the various elements of cost are identified, however, the reality becomes apparent. The cost of holding stock and work-in-progress includes:

- interest charges on the finance required
- occupancy costs such as rent, rates and any service charges for the premises
- heating and lighting of the premises
- insurance costs
- damage and theft of stock
- storage equipment and mechanical handling costs.

Effective inventory management requires continuous communication between marketing, sales, production and purchasing staff. In some companies, detailed production and purchasing budgets will be produced. One thing is certain, however, either the actual volume or mix of sales is likely to prove significantly different from budget. This requires that:

- marketing staff alert the other department to forthcoming promotional campaigns and the forecast impact on sales

- sales staff continuously notify both production and purchasing staff of changes in the volume of enquiries and orders received, so that schedules may be amended accordingly.

Every effort should be made to reduce the time of the production cycle to turn raw materials into finished goods for sale. The concept of just-in-time inventory management should be adapted by small businesses to get tangible benefits for themselves. These techniques are not the sole preserve of large companies.

Creditor payment

To delay paying creditors until legal action is commenced may be costly and counter-productive. For example, if tax is not paid by the due date, the Inland Revenue will charge interest and it is not an allowable charge against taxable profits. Some suppliers will seize any opportunity to increase the price quoted in order to compensate themselves for anticipated slow payment. When a delivery or service is required urgently, the request for help from a slow-paying customer may be met with little enthusiasm.

The ingredients for effective supplier management and creditor payment include ensuring that:

- no order is placed without an agreed price. This happens surprisingly often, especially on urgent orders, and is an invitation to the supplier to choose the price to be paid

- each order is properly authorised. A secretary may order another filing cabinet simply because the existing one is full. If the manager had known, perhaps half of the contents could have been scrapped or archived

- payment is properly authorised. The order may have been supplied, but payment needs to be authorised to confirm that the quality and performance are satisfactory

- early payment is made to benefit from attractive discounts. The benefit to be gained by taking advantage of the prompt-payment discount may be substantially more than the cost of additional overdraft interest

- quantity discounts are taken for placing large orders, with the flexibility of changing call-off rates to suit varying demand. Some suppliers offer substantial percentage discounts for large orders. The negotiation of flexible call-off rates avoids the risk of excessive stocks if the demand is lower than expected

- the budgeted creditor-payment period is adhered to on an overall basis. If the budgeted credit payment is, say, 40 days, then this will be achieved by a selective approach to the speed with which each creditor is paid.

Overhead costs

A common cause of cash-flow crisis is the creation of substantial overhead costs in anticipation of future sales, which do not result as quickly as expected. For example, the development of a major new product may be substantially more costly than expected and take considerably longer to achieve. Or the level of sales achieved from additional branches may be much lower than expected.

It is not enough simply to produce a cash-flow budget based upon optimistic sales projections. It is essential to be satisfied that sufficient finance will be available if actual sales should be considerably lower than expected.

Another trap to be avoided is when the budget is based on an ambitious and continuously increasing sales pattern throughout the year. The staff required to achieve the budgeted sales growth need to be recruited and trained to make it happen. Caution is needed with recruitment elsewhere in the business, however, because if the sales growth is less than expected, the overhead burden will be a drain on both profit and cash flow.

Adequate finance

Cash flow is difficult to predict accurately. It depends not just on the volume and timing of sales during the year, but the speed with which customers pay their invoices as well.

Safety first must be the motto. It is dangerous, not merely unwise, to assume that the finance required is simply that indicated by translating an ambitious sales budget into a cash-flow requirement. If the actual sales fall below budget, there is likely to be a disproportionate effect on profit and cash flow. This applies particularly to service companies with overhead costs which are largely fixed in short-term over a wide range of sales levels, for example an insurance broker or an estate agency.

The cash-flow consequences of a lower level of sales must be quantified, and the board must be satisfied that adequate finance is available. The sources of external finance available include:

- issuing more 'paper' such as ordinary shares; preference shares; convertible loan stock; loan stock and loan notes
- sales and leaseback of freehold properties
- leasing and hire purchase of assets
- fixed-term loans
- debt factoring
- bank overdrafts.

The options are described below.

Using 'paper'

For a private company, probably the last thing the shareholders want to do is to inject, and effectively lock up, more of their own cash by issuing additional shares. Equally, for a stockmarket-listed company the issue of more shares, either by a rights issue to existing shareholders for cash or to pay for the acquisition of a company, may result in reduced earnings per share in the short-term. The effect of this may be to reduce the market price of the shares.

Nevertheless, there has to be an acceptable balance between the amount of funds provided by the shareholders and borrowed money. This is why profit retained in the business is such an important source of finance.

Private companies should not overlook the opportunity to invite one or more financial institutions to invest in their company by buying some ordinary shares, and perhaps providing a loan as well. The cash could be used either to provide finance for expansion or to pay for the acquisition of a company, where the vendors understandably insist on receiving cash rather than shares in another unquoted company. Three or four institutions should be approached in order to secure the best terms, and they will probably insist upon the appointment of a non-executive director. Professional advice should be obtained to ensure that an attractive deal is negotiated.

Preference shares tend to be less common than ordinary shares because they are less attractive to many investors. A preference shareholder is usually entitled to receive a fixed percentage dividend, provided that sufficient profit is available to pay the dividend. Only when the preference dividend has been paid is the ordinary shareholder entitled to receive any dividend. So the ordinary shareholder suffers more risk but also has the potential to receive more reward when the company is successful.

Convertible loan stock, loan stock and loan notes are sources of finance available to the stockmarket-listed company more readily than a privately owned business. Loan stock provides investors with the opportunity to earn a fixed amount of interest, and units may be bought and sold in the same way as ordinary shares. The rate of interest payable by the company could be lower than a bank loan or overdraft in certain circumstances. Convertible loan stock would pay a lower rate of interest, but offer the investors the opportunity to convert the loan stock into ordinary shares, potentially on advantageous terms. For example, convertible loan stock issued in 1999 may:

- pay interest of 9.5% on the nominal value

- be convertible between 1 August 2011 and 31 July 2013 into ordinary shares at a price of 240p, compared with the present market price of 205p, so that if the shares are valued at more than 240p during the conversion period, there is an opportunity to buy the shares at below market price

- be redeemable for cash at the nominal value on 31 July 2015.

Loan notes may be issued by a quoted company to pay for the acquisition of a private company, at the request of the vendors, to defer the payment of capital gains tax. Normally, the loan notes will pay a fixed rate of interest, and repayment may be guaranteed by a bank.

Sale and leaseback
of freehold properties

Opportunities are often available to sell a freehold property to a financial institution and to lease it back for continued use by the business. Whilst the annual cost is likely to be lower than a bank loan secured on the freehold, the benefit of increasing property values has been given up. Also, the lease may well be subject to upwards-only rent review every five years. Nevertheless, the sale and leaseback of property is an option worthy of consideration in certain situations.

Asset leasing
and hire purchase

These sources of finance are readily available, easy to arrange and seem financially painless at the time. It is too easily forgotten, however, that the business is being burdened with quarterly payments for several years. Also, it must be assumed that the effective finance cost will be higher than a bank overdraft.

Usually there are severe penalties for early termination of the arrangements. When a motor car is no longer required, there may be a penalty of several months' costs for early termination. One company arranged a finance package for a telephone switchboard over a seven-year period. Within two years, a larger one was needed. Only then did they read the conditions attached. They had a legal obligation to continue the payments for the full seven-year period, without any right to sell or trade in the equipment in the meantime.

Debt factoring

Debt factoring involves 'selling' the outstanding debtors for an immediate payment of about 70% to 80% of their value. The balance will be paid when the debts are collected, after deducting a charge to cover the cost of the finance and service provided. Debt factoring is widely available from reputable companies, and some of them are subsidiaries of major banks. They usually carry out the collection of money from customers, and so relieve the business of another task as well. Once again, the cost involved must be compared with other options available to the company. Also, it should be noted in passing that to a conservatively minded accountant the use of debt factoring may imply that the company has borrowed excessively to some degree.

Fixed-term loans

Medium and long-term loans are available from banks and other financial institutions. The interest rate may be a fixed percentage throughout, or vary in relation to changes in the bank base rate. Capital and interest may be repayable quarterly, or merely the loan interest. Security may be required in the form of a charge on a freehold property.

Some institutions may ask for the opportunity to buy some ordinary shares in return for providing the loan. This should be resisted.

If necessary, other prospective lenders should be approached. Some people have found that they have sold some of their share capital far too cheaply, and unnecessarily, in this way.

Bank overdraft

A bank overdraft is not a permanent facility. Correctly, a bank overdraft is included in the balance sheet as a Creditor Due Within One Year. Bank overdrafts are repayable on demand, and are subject to renegotiation annually. Understandably banks do not expect an overdraft to be used as a source of permanent finance. A bank overdraft is designed to cope with the changing needs of working capital during the year. Ideally there should be times when the overdraft facility is not required.

Many owners of private businesses do not even know what rate of interest, calculated by the excess over the current percentage bank rate, is charged on their overdrafts. Not only should they find out the rate charged, but they should ask their auditor or accountant what rate they should be paying. As a business grows, and becomes financially sounder, the interest rate should be reduced. It has to be said, however, it is unusual for a bank manager to propose a reduction. One needs to ask and negotiate a competitive overdraft rate.

Monitoring cash flow

It is not acceptable simply to check the bank statement each month to be satisfied that the balance is in line with the comparable figure in the cash-flow budget. The situation may be much worse than budget because:

- some major payments, such as VAT or property rents, were paid but not cleared for payment in time to appear on the month-end statement

- the finance staff have been slowing down payments to suppliers in order to keep within the cash-flow budget or overdraft limit

- a large unscheduled payment needs to be made next month

The effective monitoring of cash flow requires:

- the actual receipts and payments to be compared with budget each month to identify differences which would otherwise remain hidden for a time

- the cash-flow forecast to be updated each month for each of the next three months and the remainder of the financial year in total to identify the need for corrective action.

In some large companies, the cash-flow forecast for the next month is prepared on a week-by-week basis for tighter cash control.

Bank contact

Some companies mistakenly adopt the policy of avoiding contact with the bank manager, wherever possible. This is short-sighted. Sooner or later, the time will come when the support of the bank is needed to help the business handle a temporary cash-flow crisis. When this happens, the goodwill created by regular communication with the bank is definitely helpful.

The minimum communication required is to telephone the bank if the overdraft limit is to be exceeded, even if only for a day. It is a basic courtesy and gives the confidence that the business knows what is happening to the overdraft. If the overdraft limit is likely to become inadequate, a meeting should be arranged to explain the circumstances and to present an up-dated monthly cash-flow forecast.

Other companies go further than this. The bank will be supplied with a copy of the audited accounts and the annual phased cash-flow budget and management accounts at intervals during the year. This is not essential. It does, however, give more confidence to the bank. It is possible, too, that the bank manager may be able to offer an alternative approach to meet the financing needs which is more attractive than an increased overdraft.

Profit management

8

The profit-driven manager must understand the anatomy of profit. Otherwise, he or she is as ill equipped to operate on profit management, as the surgeon would be to operate without a knowledge of human anatomy.

Surprisingly, perhaps, the statutory or conventional profit-and-loss account is not sufficiently revealing about the anatomy of profit. The profit-and-loss account needs to be analysed into variable and fixed costs, to show the marginal profit, for effective profit management.

Variable costs

Variable costs are those costs which increase or decrease directly pro rata to changes in sales volume. Examples of variable costs are:

- the materials used to make a product

- royalties payable on each sale

- carriage costs when using a parcels carrier rather than a company delivery fleet.

Fixed costs

Fixed costs remain unchanged in the short-term despite changes in sales volume, unless specific action is taken. These costs tend to be related to time rather than volume, such as monthly salaries and depreciation. Examples of fixed costs are:

- rent
- rates
- depreciation
- salaries
- cleaning costs.

Clearly some costs are partly variable. An obvious example is the cost of the telephones. There is a fixed charge and a variable charge. One could carry this argument to extremes, arguing that even the annual audit might be increased if the number of transactions and value of inventory were significantly higher. This would miss the point and lose the benefit to be gained from this analysis of costs.

The proportion of variable costs in relation to sales varies widely according to the type of business. The variable costs of a discount retailer, the actual product costs, will be a large percentage of sales. For a ten-pin bowling alley, the percentage of variable costs will be low. It would be wrong to assume, however, that a low proportion of variable costs will automatically create high profits and vice versa.

The profit will be affected by the level of fixed costs within the business, regardless of the level of sales achieved.

A more important issue for a manufacturing company is the classification of production labour costs. These are directly connected with the cost of the product, but not necessarily variable. Few companies recruit and terminate production staff directly in relation to sales volumes. The likelihood is that the labour force is regarded as a fixed resource in the short-term, and modest changes in sales volume are absorbed by changes in inventory levels.

For the sake of ease of calculation, some companies identify the costs which are truly variable and classify the remainder as fixed. This is not entirely accurate, but is probably sufficiently so for the purpose.

Marginal profit

Marginal profit is defined as the sales revenue minus the variable cost of sales. An important figure to know for profit management is the percentage marginal profit:

$$\frac{\text{sales revenue} - \text{variable cost of sales}}{\text{sales revenue}} \times 100$$

$$= \frac{\text{marginal profit}}{\text{sales revenue}} \times 100$$

If the sales of a company are £10.0m and the variable cost of sales is £5.5m, then the % marginal profit is:

$$\frac{£10m - £5.5m}{£10m}$$

$$= \frac{£4.5m}{£10m} = 45\%$$

It must not be assumed that a high percentage marginal profit will ensure high profits.

An extreme example illustrates what may happen. Some years ago an electronics company formed a subsidiary company to make and sell silicon chips. It was realised at the outset that the minimum viable size of the production unit and the essential number of technical staff required would lead to substantial losses in the early years. During the third financial year, a 74% marginal profit was achieved. As a result of actual sales still being much lower than the available capacity, however, the fixed costs were 205% of sales revenue. So a loss of 131% of sales resulted. In sharp contrast, the next year produced sales nearly three times higher and a modest profit was achieved.

Some managers assume that percentage marginal profit achieved by each product or service group in a business will be virtually identical. In many businesses, the reality is dramatically different. For example, if the overall average marginal profit is 45%, the figures for individual product or service groups may range from 30% to 60%, or even wider still.

Effective profit management requires maximising not just the total sales value produced from a given level of fixed costs, but maximising the total amount of marginal profit generated.

Unless the percentage of marginal profit is known for each product or service group, profit management is reduced to shooting in the dark. What is worse, customers have an uncannily accurate knack of recognising bargain prices, even if the supplier is unaware that a bargain price is being offered, which means a best-selling product or service may result from the sales price reflecting a lower-than-average percentage marginal profit.

Ignorance of marginal profit percentages can be disastrous. A computer-component manufacturer suffered a fall in selling prices from £2.25 to £0.79 in less than 18 months, because of overcapacity amongst suppliers. A once-profitable company rapidly produced heavy losses. A policy decision was taken to capture more market share to eliminate the losses. Unfortunately the losses increased further. A company doctor was called in to save the business. It was rapidly established that the variable cost was £0.89, 10 pence higher than the selling price, with little scope for improvement using the existing facilities. The company had been leap-frogged by competitors using the latest technology to reduce production costs substantially.

A knowledge of the percentage marginal profit produced by each product or service group enables the profit-driven manager to increase profit by:

- ensuring that marketing effort is biased towards the products and services producing above-average percentage marginal profit

- directing sales resources towards the above average percentage-marginal-profit lines. If appropriate, differential sales commission incentives should be introduced

- value engineering below-average products and services to increase the percentage marginal profit by reducing the variable cost where possible; and incorporating features which will command a disproportionately higher sales price as well

- making sure that any new products and services introduced will at least maintain the overall average percentage marginal profit achieved by the business.

Other ingredients of effective profit management are:

- a knowledge of the break-even point of the business

- the management of product profitability

- the profitability achieved from key customers

- the dangers of marginal pricing.

Each of these aspects will be described.

Break-even point

The break-even point of a business is the level of sales at which neither a profit nor a loss results.

A knowledge of the total fixed costs and the overall percentage marginal profit allows the break-even point to be calculated:

$$\text{Break-even point} = \frac{\text{fixed costs}}{\text{\% marginal profit}}$$

Consider a company with fixed costs of £9m and a marginal profit of 45%:

$$= \frac{\text{fixed costs}}{\text{\% marginal profit}}$$

$$= \frac{\text{£9m}}{45\%}$$

$$= \text{£20m}$$

This can be demonstrated to be correct, because a marginal profit of 45% means that the variable cost of sales is 55%, so the profit on sales of £20m is:

	£m	%
Sales	20	100
Variable cost of sales	11	55
Marginal profit	9	45
Fixed costs	9	45
Profit before tax	0	0

A change in the volume of sales, if sales prices and fixed costs remain unchanged, will have a disproportionate impact upon profits. Consider an increase or decrease in budgeted sales volume of 10%:

	Budget	10% sales increase	10% sales decrease
£m			
Sales	10.00	11.00	9.00
Variable cost of sales	5.50	6.05	4.95
Marginal profit	4.50	4.95	4.05
Fixed costs	3.70	3.70	3.70
Profit/(Loss) before tax	0.80	1.25	0.35
	= 8%	= 12.5%	= 3.5%

The higher the percentage marginal profit, the greater is the impact of a change of sales volume on the profit before tax, and vice versa.

In the example above, a 10% increase in sales volume improves the profit on sales from 8% to 12.5%. A similar decrease in sales volume reduces the profit on sales from 8% to 3.5%, unless other action is taken. It would be easy to dismiss this as correct in theory, but something that does not happen in real life. Unfortunately, that would be wrong.

Consider the company illustrated, and assume that by the end of the first quarter of the financial year it is forecast that the sales for the year will be 10% lower than the volume budgeted. The loss of marginal profit will be £450,000. The fixed costs for the remaining three-quarters of the year will be about £2.8m. About half of this amount may be staff salaries and associated costs. Clearly, it would be impossible to offset the loss of marginal profit by corresponding savings on employment costs, without serious damage to the business. A substantial shortfall of profit compared to the annual budget is probably unavoidable at this stage of the year.

The effect of sales volume on profit can be illustrated graphically:

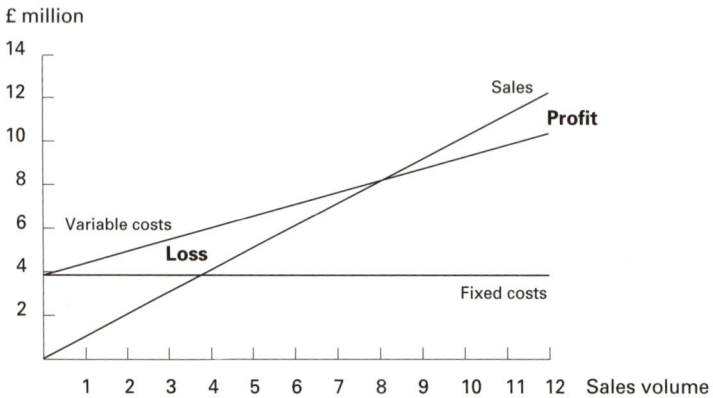

Product and service profitability

The calculation of the profit or loss before tax achieved by a product or service group involves guesswork in many businesses. The reason is that many of the staff and facilities in a complex business are shared by more than one product or service group. This means that accountants apportion or allocate a fair share of the common costs to individual products or services. Words such as 'apportion' and 'allocate' give a feel of scientific accuracy, when a degree of informed guesswork is really what is involved. As a result, the profit or loss before tax calculated for a product or service group may be significantly inaccurate.

Consider the following example:

£m	Product or service 'A'
Sales	4.8
Variable cost of sales	2.9
Marginal profit	1.9
Specific fixed costs	(0.5)
Allocated fixed costs	(1.8)
Profit/(loss) before tax	(0.4)

Only £0.5m of fixed costs are specific to 'A', in other words costs exclusively incurred for the particular product. The allocated fixed costs of £1.8m are based upon a degree of informed guesswork to arrive at a fair share of common staff and facilities costs to be attributed to 'A'.

If a decision was taken immediately to discontinue 'A' in order to eliminate the loss, the result in most businesses would be that the overall loss would increase! The reality is that it is improbable that the common fixed costs could be reduced by as much as £1.4m. As marginal profit of £1.9m would be lost by discontinuing sales of 'A', savings of at least £1.4m are needed in fixed costs which are shared by more than product 'A' in addition to the £0.5m which are specific to 'A'. Otherwise the overall profit of the company must be reduced.

Customer profitability

Customer concentration is growing. Many businesses have one or more customers each of which account for at least 5% of total invoiced sales. Quite often these customers are more demanding than less important ones. In addition to receiving lower prices or being given quantity discounts, other costs may be incurred as well. For example, special packing or delivery arrangements may be required. In a service company the more experienced and costly staff may be involved to ensure the highest standards of service for major clients.

Whenever a customer accounts for more than 5% of total sales, the percentage marginal profit for the customer should be calculated. Also, if any additional overhead costs are incurred for a particular customer, these should be identified as well. For example, one company willingly undertook product development for a major retail chain to be able to offer them exclusive designs. Financial analyses showed, however, that a totally disproportionate part of the development budget was spent on behalf of this customer. This may well have been a sound decision. The important issue is that the financial analysis should be done to ensure that the profit implication is known.

The importance of measuring customer profitability was demonstrated in the following situation. A stationery manufacturer won a major retail chain as a customer. Every product design supplied had to be exclusive in some way, so that the own-label brand of the retail was distinctively different from other brands. Until obtaining this major customer, the manufacturer had achieved little sales growth in recent years.

Within three years, the major retailer accounted for nearly one third of total sales. More importantly, however, the percentage marginal profits of the various product groups had fallen significantly except in two cases. Revealingly, these were the products not supplied to the major retailer. Belatedly, the percentage marginal profit obtained on sales to the major retailer was calculated. It was barely half of that achieved on sales to other customers. Fortunately, the retailer was keen for products to be redesigned regularly in order to maintain customer interest.

So the efforts to improve customer profitability were focused upon aggressive value engineering of the specification of new products, coupled with a determined attempt to negotiate favourable prices for them.

Marginal-pricing danger

This chapter has concentrated upon the importance of marginal-profit analysis to optimise customer, product and service profitability. Marginal pricing, in contrast, may well undermine existing profitability instead of improving it.

If there is spare capacity in a business, regardless of whether it is a manufacturer or a service company, one could argue that marginal pricing should be adopted. In other words, the surplus capacity should be sold at cut prices as long as some marginal profit is gained from each sale. Arithmetically this appears attractive, but the real dangers are:

- the cut-price work undermines the normal priced business, or even substitutes for some of it

- a price war with competitors may be sparked off and prices generally may be reduced.

If it does make sense to utilise spare capacity by accepting business with lower profitability, important aspects are to:

- limit the amount of cut-price business and the period during which it will be offered, otherwise it may be so attractive to customers that overall profitability will fall

- offer a more basic specification than normal, to justify and preserve the price differential

- direct the cut-price business towards a different type of customer or country, so that the base business is not undermined.

Financial analysis for decision-making

9

Few major business decisions are so clearcut that financial analysis can be safely ignored, because the benefits are so overwhelming. Some managers leave the financial analysis completely to an accountant. As the financial analysis could make or break the decision to proceed, this is an abdication of responsibility rather than delegation of the calculation involved.

Equally, many managers are unfamiliar with the most effective techniques of financial analysis to assist decision-making. Words such as discounted pay-back periods, internal rates of return, net present values and sensitivity analysis seem proof enough that financial analysis for decision-making is beyond the grasp of managers. Such an assumption is entirely wrong. The profit-driven manager does not even need to be able to do the calculations, because widely available and inexpensive software and even some electronic calculators will produce the answers.

Financial analysis for decision-making requires:

- a knowledge of which technique is appropriate

- forecasts of future revenues, costs and cash flows

- an understanding of the answer produced by the personal computer or calculator.

Technique

There is wide acceptance that the appropriate financial analysis technique for decision-making is based upon cash flow and not profit. Decisions should be based upon:

- future cash flows

- incremental and differential cash flows

- company-wide cash flows.

Each of these terms is sufficiently important to require further explanation.

Only future cash flows should be taken into account when making a decision.

Past and irretrievable cash flows should be ignored. This is something which some managers find hard to accept. Perhaps an illustration will help. Consider a development project to design a new aircraft engine. It has become clear that the original cost budget, on which the financial analysis was based, will be substantially exceeded. A decision is to be made whether to complete the development or abort it. It is estimated that £350m will be needed to complete the development work.

The amount spent to date, and the extent to which costs have exceeded budget, are irrelevant for decision purposes. Regardless of whether the project proceeds or not, development costs to date will have to be charged to the profit-and-loss account. The decision needs to be based upon whether or not a further outlay of £350m is justified by the cash-flow benefits to be gained from the current estimate of future sales. If the completion will be delayed significantly, allowing a competitor to bring out a rival engine, future prospects may be adversely affected.

Incremental and differential cash flow is simpler than it sounds. Cash flows which will continue whether or not the decision to proceed is made should be ignored, and only differences taken into account. Consider a decision to extend a retail shop.

The incremental and differential cash flows need to be based upon:

- cost of building work and fitting out the additional space
- extra sales expected
- additional staff required
- incremental overhead costs.

Costs which exist already and will not increase should be ignored completely, and no attempt should be made to apportion a share of these costs when doing the financial analysis for decision-making. For example, the store manager will not need to be duplicated. Only the cost of any salary increase for added responsibility should be taken into account.

The company-wide impact on cash flow must be assessed, and not merely the effect upon the department initiating the project. Consider a publishing company, organised into publishing divisions serving different market sectors, and a separate division handling warehousing and distribution. One of the divisions wishes to undertake a major project to enter the educational books market. It would be wrong for the publishing division to ignore the cash-flow implications on, for example, the warehousing and distribution division. Either a new warehouse or an extension to the existing one may be needed, involving a substantial cash outlay. This must be included in the project evaluation.

In a similar way, the requirement of additional working capital must not be overlooked. Quite often working capital is a significant part of the overall cash-flow investment in an expansion project. Corporation tax payable on profits should be taken into account as well.

Evaluation

The criteria most commonly used to evaluate the cash-flow projection for a proposed project are:

- pay-back period
- discounted pay-back period
- percentage internal rate of return
- net present value.

Each of these will be explained.

Pay-back period

This method simply calculates the time required for the incremental cash outflow to be recouped. For example, consider a project as follows:

Initial cash outlay £40,000
Annual cash inflow:

Year	
1	£5,000
2	£10,000
3	£15,000
4	£20,000
5	£10,000

Then the pay-back period is 3.5 years, as it will be halfway through the fourth year before the cumulative cash inflow equals the initial cash outflow of £40,000.

There are two obvious shortcomings of using the pay-back period for decision-making:

- interest costs on the cash outflow are ignored
- no consideration is given to either the duration or amount of cash inflow after the pay-back period.

Discounted pay-back period

The discounted pay-back method takes into account the interest costs on the cash outflow. So the discounted pay-back period is the time required to recoup the initial cash outflow, at an assumed rate of interest. No consideration of what happens afterwards is taken into account.

Some companies assume a standard rate of interest when using discounted pay-back periods, on the assumption that the current interest rate may be temporarily high or low and not typical of the likely average interest rate during the pay-back period. Also, by choosing a standard rate of interest, a minimum pay-back period can be set in order for a decision to proceed to be taken.

In the previous example, the pay-back period was 3.5 years. If a standard interest rate of 10% is assumed, the discounted pay-back period would be 4.3 years. Using a typical bank overdraft rate of, say 9%, when this book was written, the discounted pay-back period would be about four years.

Percentage internal rate of return

This is often referred to as the % IRR. If the cash flows from a project are calculated to give a 17% IRR, after tax, this means that the weighted average return, taking into account the changes in the net cash outflow which are expected to occur during the project, and calculated net of corporation tax, over the assumed effective life of the project, is 17%.

This allows a company to set a minimum % IRR for projects to be authorised. Many companies require a minimum % IRR of at least 15% net of tax.

The effective life of the project is not necessarily the useful physical life of the assets. For example, some purpose-built electronic test equipment may perform satisfactorily for at least 20 years. The effective life of the project may be only five years, however, because by then the market demand for the particular product will have expired.

Net present value

Net present value is another variation of discounted cash-flow techniques, but the most abstract one for managers to use. Generally speaking, the % IRR is much more widely used and easier to understand.

As some companies do use net present value, often abbreviated to NPV, it will be described briefly. The NPV is the net present value of all the cash outflows and inflows, discounted at a standard percentage rate chosen by the company. For example, the NPV of the cash flows in the previous example, discounted at 15%, is a net outflow of £1,280.

Such an answer seems to beg the question: is this an acceptable return or not? One method of answering this is to calculate a NPV index, defined as:

NPV index

$$= \frac{\text{NPV, at assumed rate of return}}{\text{maximum cash outflow}}$$

This still requires a second calculation, compared to the % IRR method.

Essential replacements and legislation requirements

Some important investment decisions are not necessarily suitable for financial analysis. Consider the need to increase the memory capacity of personal computers throughout a business. The existing maintenance contract may require the additional capacity to be obtained from the same supplier, so there is essentially no feasible alternative to be evaluated. The needs of business growth demand that more memory capacity is obtained. Financial analysis is not really appropriate.

Consider a different situation. Suppose there was a genuine choice between expanding the existing memory capacity or buying a completely new system, which would cost substantially more but allow worthwhile operating-cost savings to be made. The differential cost of the two alternatives can be compared with the incremental operating savings, so financial analysis is appropriate.

Legislation may require an investment decision to be made. Clearly financial analysis is inappropriate unless there is a choice available of different ways to meet the legal requirement.

Sensitivity analysis

Sensitivity analysis allows the impact of different possible outcomes to be evaluated easily. It is sometimes described as 'what if?' analysis, because it answers the question 'what if such and such were to happen?'

Typical outcomes which can be evaluated are:

■ what if development work costs 5% more than forecast?

■ what if the sales launch is delayed by six months?

■ what if sales in the first year are 10% below forecast?

■ what if sales prices are 1% higher or lower than forecast?

Various possibilities can be evaluated to find out which factors will have the greatest impact upon the return to be achieved. This allows management attention to be focused on the most sensitive aspects of the project in an informed way. An actual case concerned the building of a major chemical-process plant on a new site. The forecast was that about three years would be required from the purchase of the land to full production from the plant which was to be built. Sensitivity analysis demonstrated that if sales of the new product were delayed by more than nine months, the investment would not produce the minimum rate of return required. The reason was the substantial cost of financing the capital cost involved until the sales launch took place and operating cash flows could be generated. With the benefit of this analysis, particular attention was paid to the negotiation of no-strike agreements for the construction work involved.

The management role

The manager responsible for the project or investment must play a major part in the forecast of sales volumes, selling prices and operating costs from which the cash flows will be calculated. The accountant may well be better equipped than the manager to produce the cash-flow analysis, but must not be allowed to make assumptions about sales volumes, selling prices, staffing levels and operating costs. This is the area in which the manager must provide the requisite knowledge of the market-place and the method of operation.

Similarly, the manager should be better equipped than an accountant to know the key vulnerabilities which the project may encounter. So the manager should suggest specific 'what if'? calculations to be carried out. The accountant should carry out additional 'what if?' calculations to highlight other situations to which the rate of return would be particularly sensitive.

Equally, the manager must understand not only what the answer calculated by the accountant means, but why the company requires a given minimum rate of return. Simply to achieve a rate of return comparable with current overdraft interest rates is totally unacceptable, for several reasons:

■ managers tend to be optimistic when projecting the future cash flow to be achieved from an investment, so allowance has to be made in the rate of return required

■ occasionally, a project will fail substantially or be aborted after considerable expense has been involved

- in some businesses, about one-fifth of total investment does not generate a cash flow in return, because it is required for essential replacement, refurbishment or to meet legislation

- the effect of inflation on the purchasing value of cash during the life of the project needs taking into account

- and not least, there should be some return achieved for the benefit of shareholders to reward them for the commercial risk involved.

So it is not surprising that many companies require a rate of return of over 20% a year, before the effect of corporation tax is taken into account.

Decision audit

Some large companies demand that rigorous financial analysis is carried out for major decisions – quite rightly so, even though considerable management time is required. Then, surprisingly, they make no effort to find out how the actual return achieved compares with the projection on which the decision was made.

Admittedly, the management reporting each month is not designed to compare the actual project cash flow with the original projection. This is not even an acceptable excuse. Whenever a major investment requires the approval of a board or executive committee, it is reasonable that if the authority to proceed is given, dates should be set for occasional project-status reports to be submitted. It is important, but quite inadequate, merely to be satisfied that initial cash outflow is in line with the projection. The major uncertainty concerns the level of sales and profits achieved in the marketplace. So it could make sense to require *ad hoc* reports:

- after three months, to demonstrate that the initial costs were acceptable

- after the first year of sales, to be satisfied that the commercial and cash-flow success are in accordance with the original projection for this period.

The introduction of decision-audit reports tends to have a significant effect upon managers submitting investment proposals. When it is known that the operational success of the project will be monitored, there tends to be a sobering effect on optimistic forecasts which might be made in a misguided attempt to demonstrate that an acceptable rate of return is to be achieved.

Investment risks and rewards

Many companies set one required rate of return for all investment situations regardless of the differing risks and uncertainties involved. This has the merit of simplicity. It could result, however, in decisions to:

- reject projects such as an investment to reduce existing costs, where there is a minimum of risk and uncertainty, because the return falls a bit short of the required minimum

- approve projects which are speculative, such as an investment to launch a new product in an overseas market.

Merchant bankers and financial institutions thoroughly understand the need for there to be an acceptable balance between potential risk and reward. They practise it too. Different rates of return are required on investment in management buy-outs compared with venture-capital finance for newly formed companies. The reason is revealing.

Actual experience demonstrates that seven or eight out of ten investments in management buy-outs are successful. So institutions seek a compound annual return in the region of 25% to 30% a year. Start-up capital is different. Two out of ten investments are likely to be outstandingly successful. Two are likely to result in outright failure. The remainder are likely to achieve varying degrees of success, and some of them only after an additional injection of finance. If only it were possible to predict the outstandingly successful investments, but it is not. So not surprisingly, the institutions seek a higher compound annual return of up to about 60% to 80% a year. Despite these substantially different rates, the actual returns achieved from management buy-outs have compared favourably with the returns from start-up capital finance.

A small proportion of large companies adopt a similar approach by setting different rates of return according to the degree of risk involved in various categories of projects. Possible categories are:

- improved efficiency on existing business, eg. investment in automation, mechanical handling, improved test facilities

- expansion of existing products or services in existing markets and countries, eg. an investment to expand an existing chilled-food business already established in Holland

- diversification into either a new product or service in an existing market or country, or vice versa, eg. a UK insurance company investing to launch a business to sell their products in Italy

- a new product or service in a new market or country, eg. a UK defence-radar company investing in a business to launch a small-boat radar product in the US market.

Clearly, the rate of return required should increase in each of the above categories. To set differential rates of return requires considerable expertise. Nevertheless, there is a case for adopting a somewhat flexible approach, even if somewhat subjectively, to investment decision-making. Low-risk projects perhaps should be approved even if the required return is not quite demonstrated. In contrast, an investment which involves considerable diversification and only just achieves the required return, requires the utmost scrutiny and should probably be rejected.

Application

The cash-flow-analysis techniques described in this chapter are widely applicable. They can be used to evaluate:

■ lease v buy decisions. The cost of outright purchase and the regular lease payments can be compared to calculate the % IRR (internal rate of return), which is the effective percentage annual cost of leasing

■ make v buy decisions. The differential cash flows of making in-house compared with buying the product or service are used to calculate the % IRR

■ expansion projects. The cash outflow required to finance capital expenditure and working capital is compared with the incremental cash inflow produced throughout the assumed project life to calculate the % IRR

■ company acquisitions. The cost of acquisitions compared with the total incremental cash-flow benefit to the acquirer to calculate a % IRR.

Commercial factors

It must never be forgotten that an acceptable rate-of return calculation is not sufficient to justify an investment decision. In addition, the proposed investment needs to be:

■ consistent with the chosen corporate strategy and commercial rationale of the business

■ the most suitable method to achieve the required goal, after consideration of the different alternatives available

■ an acceptable balance between potential reward and interest risk

■ acceptable to customers, suppliers and staff, where appropriate.

part

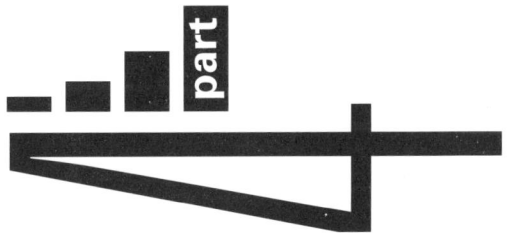

How to achieve dramatic growth in profits

Business
development

10

In the competitive world of today, a profit-driven manager cannot afford to rely merely upon a flow of bright ideas being produced to develop business successfully. A more structured approach is needed. Important ingredients for effective business development include:

- a vision statement

- a quantum-leap approach

- taking stock of the business and its markets

- identifying and evaluating the strategic options available

- organisation structure

- business-development projects, with set milestones of achievement

- the use of strategic workshops.

Each of these will be described.

Vision statement

Some managers may be more familiar with mission statements. A vision statement is somewhat different. Some mission statements tend to be so bland that they are little more than statements of parenthood. Companies could swop mission statements with each other in some cases, because they are so generalised.

A vision statement should describe the particular company in say, five years' time. In industries with long lead times, however, such as telecommunications and oil exploration, a longer timescale will be necessary. The essence is that the timescale chosen should be long enough to achieve major change. A vision could be compared to a dream, describing the future success of the company, but with the belief and commitment of the executive team to make it into a reality.

The vision should harness and focus the energies of people towards the chosen goals, and set priorities where appropriate.

A vision statement is markedly different from a business plan, which is necessarily detailed and supported by financial schedules. A vision statement should be written on one side of A4 paper. Senior executives should remind themselves of the goals by referring to it regularly, in contrast to many business plans that are quickly filed and forgotten about.

A vision statement should include and set out concisely:

- the market segments and countries to:
  - achieve, maintain or enhance market leadership in
  - continue investing in without achieving market leadership
  - enter, by organic growth or acquisition as appropriate
  - cut back, rationalise or exit from

- the commercial rationale of the company
    - to describe how the company will be seen by customers and prospective customers as attractively and distinctively different from competitors, for example:
        - all products in our supermarkets will be own-label brand; providing a comparable quality and specification with the leading branded product at a lower price, or better quality at the same price, or wherever possible an innovative product not available elsewhere and priced competitively
        - each do-it-yourself superstore will contain a garden centre, offer a home-delivery service, and provide adequate technical advice for customers upon request

- essential policies and qualitative goals which will be pursued, for example:
    - head office will act as investment banker, be as small as possible, and each subsidiary will be an autonomous business
    - sufficient investment will be made in information technology, or robotics, etc. to provide a competitive advantage in the market-place compared with competitors
    - wherever possible, each member of staff will be rewarded by an incentive scheme based upon personal achievement
- broad financial-performance goals, for example:
    - a minimum or average percentage increase in earnings per share each year
    - the proportion of total profits to be achieved from, say, the USA within the next five years
    - the percentage return to be achieved on total operating assets within five years

- future ownership (this is particularly relevant for private companies and professional partnerships), for example:

    - a stockmarket listing will be obtained within the next three years

    - a merger with another partnership will be pursued to ensure that adequate technical support is affordable.

The examples described above are from actual vision statements. This does not necessarily suggest that these examples are appropriate for other companies to adopt.

Copies of the vision statement in a business should be restricted to directors, partners and senior executives because it is highly confidential. Nevertheless, the relevant parts of the vision can be communicated orally to management and staff as part of briefing meetings. A vision statement is helpful in recruiting the most talented executives and technical specialists. Whilst it is not appropriate to provide a copy of the vision statement at the selection stage, reference to the vision will demonstrate that the company is committed to success.

Quantum leap approach

Belief in, and commitment to, the achievement of the vision are much more important for success than sophisticated corporate planning techniques. Aspiration and attitude are all important.

In contrast, some managers simply plan to achieve mediocrity, and then do not manage to achieve it. How? By planning for only a modest improvement in results, when this amounts to nothing more than continued mediocrity.

The profit-driven manager is committed to achieving a quantum leap in results as a vital part of the vision.

A quantum leap is a dramatic improvement, without any significant increase in the commercial risks to be undertaken. Quantum leaps are not achieved in a week or a month, and probably not even in a year. Initiatives can be made during this week, this month and this year, however, which will result in a quantum leap being achieved within the medium term.

The ability to achieve a quantum leap is limited only by the imagination. The results achieved are more likely to fall short of the ambition, rather than exceed it. Imagination alone is not enough. To achieve a quantum leap requires:

- belief – that it can and will be achieved

- commitment – to make the effort needed to make it happen

- persistence – to overcome setbacks and obstacles which will be encountered

- enthusiasm – to help motivate people.

The motto might be 'think big and make it happen!' The growth and success of companies such as Microsoft, Nissan and MacDonalds did not happen by accident.

The first step for a small business to become a national or worldwide market leader is for the chief executive to have the vision, belief and total commitment to make it happen.

Taking stock

This means taking stock of present performance, comparing it with leading competitors where appropriate, and the market opportunities available. Objective measurement is needed, a comfortable view of performance seen through rose-tinted spectacles is inappropriate.

Facets of performance and market opportunities which should be assessed include:

- actual and forecast percentage market shares

- percentage share of each distribution channel within a market

- attractive opportunities in different market segments and countries

- benefits and performance of each product or service group

- niche market opportunities which exist or could be created, for example: weekend hotel breaks to cater for special-interest groups such as those interested in gourmet food, wine tasting, antique collecting, bridge, clay-pigeon shooting, etc.

- gaps in the range of products or services offered

- overall percentage return on operating assets

- pricing and discount structures

- identification of major non-customers, especially in markets where there is a concentration of major customers such as supermarket groups and do-it-yourself superstore chains

- speed of delivery and the provision of after-sales service

- level of warranty claims or complaints, and the speed of handling them

- value of business lost by an inability to supply quickly enough

- opportunities to subcontract or out-source services more cost effectively than providing them in-house, such as vehicle-fleet management, staff catering, pension administration, cleaning, physical distribution, specialist tax advice, etc.

- level of research and development expenditure, and the results achieved

- staff retention levels.

The aim of this assessment should be to identify:

- opportunities available within the existing business which should be capitalised upon

- attractive niche markets which can be created out of the existing business

- different market segments and countries which should be entered

- the opportunity or need for selective price changes

- the need to set and to achieve improved standards of performance and to reduce costs.

Strategic options

A quantum leap in achievement requires that the strategic options are identified and evaluated. Furrow management, which is merely pursuing minor variations of the same theme, is the enemy of the quantum leap.

Strategic options need to be identified and evaluated for the overall business and within each major department of the business. For example, strategic options at the corporate level of a listed company may include:

- acquiring a larger company overseas to achieve a significant local market share quickly

- obtaining a stockmarket listing in one or more overseas countries in which the company has a substantial business

- obtaining a separate stockmarket flotation for a major subsidiary, and retaining an equity stake, which would command a higher price-earnings ratio than the group as a whole

- transferring the freehold properties into a separate company and obtaining a stockmarket listing for it

- joining with an overseas competitor to make a bid for a major group, where only parts of the business are relevant to acquire

- pursuing a management buy-out of the stockmarket-listed group in the face of an unwelcome and hostile bid from a corporate raider.

Strategic options which should be evaluated to improve the marketing efforts of a professional partnership may include:

- recruiting a marketing director from outside the profession

- producing a corporate brochure for the first time

- appointing a public-relations consultancy to obtain press and magazine coverage

- presenting seminars to an invited audience of clients and prospective clients on subjects of topical interest that could create business opportunities

- inviting selected clients and prospective clients to lunch to discuss a subject related in some way to the services provided

- encouraging staff to write technical articles for publication in relevant magazines

- experimenting with arts or sports sponsorship on a selective basis

- establishing personal contact with firms in different professions who are in a position to introduce business.

These examples are not recommendations for general use. The intention is to illustrate the range of strategic options which can be identified and evaluated in most business situations. Furrow management must be firmly rejected, and can be easily done by throwing away a self-imposed mental straitjacket.

Organisation structure

The organisation structure of a business is important for future success. The effect of organisation structure is rarely neutral. It is likely either to help the achievement of the vision, or to hamper progress and to encourage internal politics.

A problem is that organisational changes become necessary or desirable from time to time. So several piecemeal changes may be made to the structure over a period of time. As a result, the organisation structure should be reviewed comprehensively about every three years.

There is no such thing as an ideal organisation structure, not even within a particular industry. The organisation structure needs to be designed to help the achievement of the vision and to reflect the strategic options to be pursued.

Important features to be incorporated in an effective organisation structure include:

■ the role and added value of the head office clearly defined; and the smallest number of people employed to achieve those

■ individual businesses created to serve particular market segments, rather than based upon separate product or service groups which may result in several subsidiaries serving, and even competing for, the same customer

■ each business responsible for profit, with control of marketing and selling

■ personal accountability for achieving measurable results throughout the business.

When the organisation structure has been redesigned to achieve the vision and strategic options selected, the strengths and weaknesses of key individuals should be taken into account. Some changes may be needed to capitalise on the strengths of certain people and to compensate for their weaknesses. The aim must be to produce an organisation structure that meets the business need and makes the best use of people. Occasionally, however, it may be necessary to recruit someone externally to fill a newly created key appointment rather than compromise by relying upon candidates from within.

People talk about the loneliness of the chief executive of any business. A real example of this is the creation of a new organisation structure. Involving members of the executive team to design a new structure may cause problems arising from self-interest. Organisation change often means that some people will gain in seniority and importance, whilst others will lose. If the chief executive of a business wants to involve other people, the choice should probably be restricted to the chairman, the group chief executive where appropriate, the human resources director, non-executive directors or outside consultants to guard against vested interests and resistance to change.

Business-development projects

Revolution is a dangerous recipe for corporate success. In many businesses, with the severity of competition increasing faster than customer demand, evolution is likely to be equally dangerous. What is more, evolution alone is likely to be totally inadequate to achieve a quantum leap.

A proven way to drive a business forward is to create and to pursue vigorously a handful of business-development projects.

Each project should be the specific accountability of a member of the board or executive committee. Tangible milestones of achievement should be set to ensure adequate progress within the next 12 months. The capital expenditure, working capital and operating costs connected with each project should be included in the approved annual budget, to ensure that adequate resources will be made available.

The business-development projects should not be restricted to research and development. They should focus on whatever achievement is vital to the achievement of the vision and a quantum leap. Projects could be concerned with any aspect of the business, for example:

- entry into an overseas market by the appointment of distributors

- a company-wide attack on quality, because sustained and critical comment in the press has seriously affected sales

- the acquisition of a silicon-chip-manufacturing company to eliminate the reliance on outside suppliers for circuits which are an essential feature of products made by the company.

Some business-development projects will be long-term. They may address opportunities which rely upon future developments in advanced technologies such as artificial intelligence, biotechnology and space-satellite broadcasting. Nevertheless, milestones of progress need to be set and achieved within the next 12 months to ensure that the requisite urgency is maintained. In businesses achieving only mediocre results, however, the business-development projects are likely to focus more upon short-term improvement.

Strategic workshops

Clearly, the structured approach to business development that has been described requires the commitment and involvement of every member of the board or executive committee. Strategic workshops are a powerful means to achieve this.

A strategic workshop should involve the board or executive committee of the business. The aim is to address those issues which are vital to future success. These could include the creation of a vision for success; setting the size of the quantum leap to be achieved; taking stock of the business and market opportunities, evaluating strategic options and creating business-development projects.

Strategic workshops should be held away from company offices, to avoid distraction by day-to-day matters. A country-house hotel is a suitable venue. Preferably, the participants will meet for dinner the evening before the workshop commences in earnest. This provides an opportunity for the chief executive to set the scene and ensures that a prompt start will be made in the morning. Two working days is probably the amount of time required to address the agenda of vital issues for success.

Features which help to achieve a productive strategic workshop include:

- an agenda restricted to issues of strategic importance; lesser matters must be ruthlessly excluded

- pre-circulated and concise 'position papers' to provide the background to each item on the agenda

- skilled chairmanship to ensure that people say what they believe, whilst avoiding excessive personal criticism

- a summary of agreement reached, decisions made and further action committed, circulated promptly after the workshop.

Strategic workshops:

- create belief and commitment to the achievement of the vision, with a clear sense of collective accountability

- improve teamwork and motivation

- are an effective management-development method to help functional directors and executives to develop a broader outlook on the overall needs of the business.

It is important that the first strategic workshop held in a business is productive, because otherwise people are likely to be less enthusiastic on the next occasion. Strategic workshops are deceptively complex, and previous experience is valuable. Consequently, some companies have used outside advice on the first occasion to ensure success. A typical role of an outside adviser would be to:

- interview each participant to identify the crucial issues for success that should be part of the agenda

- agree the agenda with the chief executive

- advise upon the format and content of the position papers

- participate during the workshop to ensure that the issues are addressed rigorously, and that positive decisions are taken and further action agreed.

Many large companies use strategic workshops in each separate subsidiary, as well as holding them at group level. Some companies go further, and use strategic workshops within major functions of subsidiary companies selectively. Strategic workshops have been widely used in professional partnerships, restricting attendance either to the management committee of the whole business or the relevant partners in a particular country or regional office.

Glossary

Annual report

This contains the:

- chairman's statement
- report of the directors of the business
- statement of accounting policies
- audited profit-and-loss account, balance sheet, and source-and-application-of-funds statement
- notes to the accounts, providing supplementary information
- in the case of stockmarket-listed companies, often includes historical performance figures over the past five or ten years

Depreciation

is the charge made to the profit-and-loss account, and the similar reduction in the asset value shown in the balance sheet, to reflect the value of an asset used up. Depreciation is frequently calculated on a 'straight-line basis'. The cost, less any estimated realisable value on disposal, is divided by the estimated number of years of the useful life of the asset.

Finance leases

are leases for the purchase of fixed assets. The monthly or quarterly payment includes an amount towards the purchase cost of the asset and the balance is the interest cost of the finance provided.

Goodwill

arises when a company is acquired at a cost greater than the value of the net assets obtained. Some companies include goodwill as an intangible asset on the balance sheet, and depreciate it over several years. Provided that sufficient reserves exist on the balance sheet, however, many companies prefer to write off goodwill immediately against reserves.

Another source of goodwill may arise when brand names are obtained by acquiring a company, but not when these are created internally. A small, but growing, number of companies have attributed a value to the brand names acquired in the balance sheet, which has the benefit of reducing the amount of goodwill to be written off against reserves.

Intangible assets

are items capitalised on the balance sheet by some companies, in addition to tangible fixed assets such as land and buildings, equipment and motor vehicles. Examples of intangible assets are goodwill, purchased brand names, research and development, and intellectual property purchased such as patents.

Nominal value

of a share is the 'face value' shown on the share certificate and is used to value the issued share capital shown in the balance sheet.

Rights issue

is an issue of shares for cash made to existing shareholders, pro rata to their existing holding of shares. For example, a 1 for 4 rights issue means that each shareholder is entitled to buy one additional share for every four already owned. In the case of a listed company, the shareholder has the opportunity to sell the rights, rather than buy the additional shares, and would receive any surplus value of the market price of the shares compared with the rights-issue price.

Share options

are granted to directors, executives and staff in many stockmarket-listed and private companies. Usually, there is a minimum period of several years before the option can be exercised and the shares actually purchased. Share options are issued at a fixed price, so that any increase in share value benefits the option holder.

Subsidiary company

is a company between 50% and 100% of which is owned by a holding company, which means that effective management control is exercised.

Tax credit

When a dividend is paid to a shareholder, an amount equal to the standard rate of income tax is deducted as a tax credit in the UK. This means that the standard rate of income tax is automatically deducted in the same way as applies to building-society interest.

Hawksmere – focused on helping you improve your performance

Hawksmere plc is one of the UK's foremost training organisations. We design and present more than 450 public seminars a year, in the UK and internationally, for professionals and executives in business, industry and the public sector, in addition to a comprehensive programme of specially tailored in-company courses. Every year, well over 15,000 people attend a Hawksmere programme. The companies which use our programmes and the number of courses we successfully repeat reflect our reputation for uncompromising quality.

Our objective for each delegate

At Hawksmere we have one major aim – that every delegate leaves each programme better equipped to put enhanced techniques and expertise to practical use. All our speakers are practitioners who are experts in their own field: as a result, the information and advice on offer at a Hawksmere programme is expert and tried and tested, practical yet up-to-the-minute.

Our programmes span all levels, from introductory skills to sophisticated techniques and the implications of complex legislation. Reflecting their different aims and objectives, they also vary in format from one day multi-speaker conferences to one and two day seminars, three day courses and week long residential workshops.

For a catalogue of our full range of courses, please call Hawksmere Customer Services on 0171 824 8257 or fax on 0171 730 4293.

Thorogood – the publishing business of the Hawksmere Group

Thorogood publishes a wide range of books, reports, special briefings and videos. Listed below is a selection of key titles.

The Masters in Management series

Mastering business planning and strategy
Paul Elkin • £19.95

Mastering financial management
Stephen Brookson • £19.95

Mastering leadership
Michael Williams • £19.95

Mastering negotiations
Eric Evans • £19.95

Mastering people management
Mark Thomas • £19.95

Mastering project management
Cathy Lake • £19.95

The Desktop Guide series

The finance and accounting desktop guide for the non-financial manager
Ralph Tiffin • £15.99

The credit controller's desktop guide
Roger Mason • £15.99

The company director's desktop guide
David Martin • £15.99

The company secretary's desktop guide
Roger Mason • £15.99

Business Action Pocketbooks · _edited by David Irwin_

Building your business pocketbook   £10.99

Developing yourself and your staff pocketbook   £10.99

Finance and profitability pocketbook   £10.99

Managing and employing people pocketbook   £10.99

Sales and marketing pocketbook   £10.99

The Essential Guide series

The essential guide to buying and selling unquoted companies
Ian Smith · £25

The essential guide to business planning and raising finance
Naomi Langford-Wood and Brian Salter · £25

The essential business guide to the Internet
Naomi Langford-Wood and Brian Salter · £19.95

Other titles

The John Adair handbook of management and leadership
edited by Neil Thomas · £19.95

The inside track to successful management
Dr Gerald Kushel · £16.95

The pension trustee's handbook (2nd edition)
Robin Ellison · £25

The handbook of management fads
Steve Morris · £8.95

The art of headless chicken management
Elly Brewer and Mark Edwards · £6.99

If you would like to order any of these titles or would like more information, please call the Customer Services department on **0171 824 8257** or fax on **0171 730 4293**.